NOTES FROM A DEVELOPING DAD

Laughs, Loves and Epic Fails From a Well Meaning but Overmatched Man.

Joe Medler

For Charlie, Teddy and Karen, without whom my life would lack all wonder and all magic...

Table of Contents

5 Ways My Kids Made Me

Kids break you. Convinced of your invincibility and imbued with the quiet confidence you have that all the voices saying it changes everything were just the subtle sounds of lesser mortals struggling through that which you will navigate better, you go forth and multiply. Then you are in bliss. Then all hell breaks loose. You are in the eye of the storm, and its destructive power only amplifies its epic beauty. You are broken. Like a wild stallion finally being ridden, you are completely under the control of your miniscule master. Before long he takes an apprentice. One whose natural tendencies to rule all that he surveys are even stronger. Before long you are melted and ready to be poured into the crucible that is designed by the needs of your overseers who act without care for your opinions or your druthers. If you are not yet ready to be poured into the mold of the life that you will lead that is no bother to them. They simply turn up the heat evermore until you are suitably pliable. They do this by nature, whose design they are bound to follow.

Some day you will wake up and discover a remnant from a former life. Perhaps its coins from a faraway land or a ticket stub to a Phish concert or that t-shirt you caught from the t-shirt gun at the ballgame. Or perhaps your high tops you bought because you'd always played basketball and always needed a pair, but they are still in perfect, fresh out of the box condition. Could be as simple as a lighter. Slowly you will realize that the memories these items bring to mind, if any, are of a person that looks a little like you and it definitely happened, but you can't relate to that person anymore. The memories are fading at the edges and you suspect that each time they spring up from now until the end they will be slightly more fuzzy. Some will disappear. Some must have done so already.

These changes are certainly the evidence of the transformation you've gone through in the course of becoming a parent to someone. Much of the change is lamentable because life is wonderful and it ends and this is more evidence that you have traveled more of that road than you wish. But the other thing you notice is that you are happy on this stretch of road. You feel like this is the most meaningful and purposeful stretch you'll travel. The defining portion of the journey and your grateful to be here. When you take stock of where you are you realize, at least I have, that I'm utterly thankful to my kids for forcing me to grow up. Forcing me to change. The changes they've prompted in me are all for the better.

These are the 5 aspects of me that have been formed by my kids that are most important to me at this moment, but don't ever think this list is complete. Were you to ask me tomorrow I could come up with a different and equally impactful list. But for now, these are the things I've learned from raising my sons to this point that I'm eternally grateful for...

1. **Failure isn't final**- My kids are growing from little bowls of jelly into fully functioning little people capable of everything from pooping on the potty to planning and executing plots of deviousness that put to shame that which I could ever pull off. In the course of doing so they are prone to encounter failure. Repeatedly. Yet, they never EVER give up. In doing this they have put me to the test as well, and it turns out I learn more from doing the wrong thing then I ever do when I get it right. Failure makes me better, a concept I lost sight of as a free floating adult. But now that I'm tethered to these little loves I'm bound to fail and persist for as long as I can imagine. It's very exciting to know defeat is a starter's gun and not a finish line.

2. **Truly unconditional love**- It's a romantic notion that we are taught to think is what we are looking for in a mate. And for its purpose of helping us understand love, it's good. But it isn't real. Also, it shouldn't be. Unconditionally loving anyone other

than your kids and your parents, if you are lucky as I am, is a myth or it's a problem. I love my wife fully, romantically, practically and perpetually. She is the love of my life. But unconditionally is dangerous. But your kids, there's no thought or deciphering needed. It's truly a feeling, beyond the ability of words to explain, and it's awesome.

3. **How to Cry**- It's not a thing guys do all that much. Perhaps at funerals, but as a young man not even then. Then you get older and perhaps a movie might touch a nerve for you. For me it's the movie 'Glory'. Gets me literally every time. But now, with the kids (not to mention I'm an old dad and I suspect I have a vastly diminishing store of testosterone) I'm able to access depths of emotions, even if I still don't really understand them, that I never could reach before. Now, I can cry just from feeling 'emotional'. It's something I would have dreaded before. Turns out it makes me feel more connected. It feels great.

4. **How to understand my own parents more deeply**- Are you kidding me!? My parents had six kids. SIX KIDS! I'm barely treading water with two. Two great ones I might add. How did I spend my twenties you ask? Whining and moaning about the lack of attention we middle kids got. I can't believe how much I couldn't see of all they did for me until I was

in this position. Now I can't find enough microphones to express to the world how amazing my life is because I was blessed with two such wonderful, generous, kind, warm, smart and funny parents as mine. Had I not had kids I'd have never understood this. At least not until it was too late.

5. **How to stop worrying and live for the moment-** People can get real crazy in the middle section of life. There's pressure from all directions in regard to all things; family, finances, work. It can make you freeze up if you have a moment to think. But whenever it gets to be too much, all I have to do is have some time with the kiddos. They are magically able to remove all worries about all that isn't right there in front of them, and this trait is remarkably contagious.

For these and many more reasons I find myself forever indebted to these tiny dictators that first went about breaking me only to build a better stronger version. Or maybe this is all a very simple version of the Stockholm syndrome.

Starry Starry Night

A story about how I met their mother...

I had an argument with my wife this morning. And last night. Well, to say it was an argument implies it was more than it was. An argument comes earlier in a relationship and it involves lots of shouting, the stating of hurtful and judgmental opinions and the generalized threat that one or both members of the pairing are on some level considering whether or not the partnership is one that is even worth saving. That's an argument.

What we have now is much more targeted and it never, well rarely, threatens the existence of an 'Us'. Our attacks now are straight to the point. We know our target and we strike in a way we know will cause the most damage while taking the least time and effort. It's the efficiency one finds in a marriage, this ability to have a full-fledged fight based on two sentences, one each and then targeted silence and muted sneers. It's not altogether bad, it's just the standard. It passes fast and allows us the opportunity to breathe and get our heads and to apologize after we acknowledge our part in causing any tension. It's also a reminder that this thing we have requires more than a little effort and growth on both of our parts.

I should mention that today was totally my fault. I have somehow allowed my new computer to become infected and in the course of trying to fix it myself have seemingly crippled it. My emotions are usually measured and tempered, not too high not too low. That said, they are irrational when it comes to these things. Or rather this specific thing. I don't know how to live without my internet which updates my podcasts efficiently entertains my sports obsessiveness and allows me to manage my various fantasy teams. My patience in its absence has all the maturity of a, well, 13 week old. That said, he was all smiles this morning and he didn't have internet either, so maybe I regress even further.

The snide nature of our tension today was my fault.

I bring this up because something else dawned on me. It's April 15th!! Isn't that WONDERFUL! Not because it's tax day, at least traditionally, or because it's a day to remember the tragic end of Abraham Lincoln, the Greatest American. These things certainly make the 15th a day to be noted. Neither of these reasons however is why I think of this day in such a positive light.

Four years ago the 15th was a cold, grey and rainy day in NYC. I lived in Astoria, Queens at the time and with my roommate ceding the TV room to me I spent the day curled up on the couch watching old movies. I specifically remember Chinatown. A unique cinematic experience if there ever was one. It was the kind of day when being on the couch and getting absorbed into the muted and faded Technicolor of a seventies indie film was the best form of getting cozy. The weather was dreadful and I could have stayed there all day. But I couldn't. I had a date that night. It was at 8. It was at Doc Watson's a bar on the upper east side, in the neighborhood where the girl I hadn't met yet lived.

When she emailed to see if we were still on (It was really quite bad out weather wise and frankly she'd been on enough of these dates to not be bothered if she missed one) I decided that heading out and meeting her was in fact the best thing to keep me from melting to the couch and succumbing to my inclination to snuggle in for the night at 2pm. She, being polite decided, okay, she'd see me there at 8. She wanted to know if I wanted to talk on the phone. I knew the reasons. Women are right to be scared of men. We're capable of scary aggression, and she couldn't have known then that I wasn't that type of guy. But I still had to say no. Really, there's nothing more awkward than that conversation, one where she's trying to pretend that she's not interrogating you and you trying to sound genuine while aware the whole time that she is trying to determine what type of man you are and whether or not she should have the top of the pepper spray flipped. So instead I gave her my cell number and told her to gimme a text if she was so inclined. I told her that I'd be happy to have a phone convo, but if it was all the same can we skip it. I hate the phone. She was cool with that.

She asked how she'll recognize me and I said that I'd wear something slutty. It was a risk, but I gotta be me and I thought it was funny. Thankfully, so did she.

We met and before she even had a beer we got away from the overcrowded Irish pub and we were both smiling, ear to ear for the whole night. Even when the bar we wound up at locked its doors and kept serving us until the wee hours, as the bartender got plowed and kept giving us and another couple down the bar from us drink after drink. We kept smiling when a little buzzed and over confident I asked her if I could kiss her, like really kiss her. We smiled through that, and the kiss still worked. We smiled all the way though telling each other how we got to this place, our mid-thirties and transplanted upstaters living and working in NYC. We smiled as we told each other our different but equally amusing stories of all the bad blind dates we'd had lately. We smiled when we realized that not only was she facing me as I sat at the bar, her free hand rested naturally and lovingly on my leg. We laughed our way through the walk to her corner, a far enough escort on a first date and we stopped long enough to be wildly inappropriate in our public display of affection on the corner of 72nd and York.

The storm we ventured out in that night was epic. It even continued into the next day and the subways could not run due to flooding. That's a rarity for the NYC transit system, believe it or not. But while we sat there falling in love, both having come in from the storm, the clouds broke and the skies cleared and we were able to walk away together, under a starry sky, hand in hand, smiling and laughing.

The 5 Stages of Moving to the Toddler Room

There is no overstating the grief one feels in moments like these. All we have in this world is love. We are born alone and we will die alone. I shout in the void and pray for the response that never comes. I haven't yet come to fully accept what is clearly to be, but it is clearly to be. What we are facing is not unique, but the feelings, the inevitable sadness and loss. These, my friend are universal. We all have or will face something devastating. Something will make each of us heartsick, not wanting to move on from a moment we can't acknowledge. To acknowledge it would only confirm that it really happened.

My loss, like many before, will follow a similar progression as it makes its way purposefully to a place where it can be turned to acceptance. Where I can move on. Today my baby, my sweet little Teddy, will be moved up to the toddler classroom in daycare. I share with you now what I have learned from the ages, and from Elisabeth Kubler Ross. I do it not for me, but to add my voice to the ages in hopes that what I experience, documented thoughtfully, may help my fellow kin in the human play in which we are all actors.

The following is partly my experience to now and partly a projection of how I presume my life will be for the days, possibly week/s to come.

Denial - I know they say he has to move classrooms and that he's literally a threat to the safety of the babies in the room, but I'm sure if I drop him off in the same class as normal no one will say anything. Besides, I think it's what they really want me to do. In fact he's been running in on his own for months now, maybe I'll just open the door far enough to let him sneak in on his own, then keep walking. He won't care. It's probably a joke anyway.

Anger - Seriously? Seriously. It's one almost 2 year old. And he's gorgeous. So he's a little 'bitey.' That's just how they play at that age. I'm surprised you didn't know that. Whatever. You're the same person that thinks he should move up to another class. Do you even know that he's INCAPABLE of being prepped for this and he's gonna be confused and terrified! Jeez, play one damn game of ding-dong-ditchyourkidinaclassyouwereclearlytoldnotto with you people and you get all sensitive.

Bargaining - Listen, I'm really sorry about that whole ditching the baby in your class thing. I actually couldn't make it out before you were opening the door to find me.

I was hiding with his older brother around the corner when you came out. I feel like such a fool. In my defense I was so mortified by this whole transition that I've been having a lot of late nights and drinking quite a bit. I honestly must not have been thinking straight. Whaddya say, you know, for Teddy's sake, we just give it until the New Year? Then I'll insist he goes, even if you don't want him to. Think about it. It really is probably the best thing for everyone.

Depression - I mixed beer with milk last night and slept in the car so the kids wouldn't wake up from the wailing. My kid is in a room all day with kids bigger then him, sleeping for the first time on a mat and not in a crib, and if he's anything like me at this moment he's scared, confused, gassy from milk beer, crying loudly in the back of a station wagon in his driveway.

Acceptance - I don't know why people worry about this kinda stuff. It's not a big deal, really. You'd think they'd get used to it. I'll be sure to give younger parents an earful when they're acting crazy about these things, tell them to relax and just go with it. It's not that hard really.

Museum Pieces

The display is nearing completion. There are a few pieces left to be completed, logged, inspected and displayed. This exhibition is of my most productive period and will be in permanent residence in the grand hall. The room, the central hub and featured showroom has been closed to all visitors for nearly four years. That's how long it has taken to produce and display the items that are to be featured. There has been a great deal of buzz generated by myself, the curator and a collaborator on this project, but the room itself has hosted only those crucial to the process. The grand hall in the museum of my life will be hosting the display, 'Our Family; The Early Years.'

I'm forever curating the museum of my life. There is endless detritus that is logged once, noted and recorded for historical purposes and donated or outright given to others or placed in the cold, dark, vast warehouse of forgotten details and mementos. Of those items that I choose to display they are ordered by importance and their prestige is evident in how I choose to display them.

This room will feed me and fuel me through the times that lie ahead. Times that will so devastate me that they will make me wonder what all this was for. My aim is to curate an exhibit so stunning, so perfectly designed for my audience of one, for me, that I will be so enamored of it as to be unable to wander too far from it. That my compulsive need to gaze on the wonders of the world that were made just for me will hard wire the memories and the feelings that drove me to complete such an ambitious, albeit not groundbreaking, body of work. I will wallow in it, work in it and invest energy in keeping it pristine. All of this in the hopes that even in my feeblest state I'll always know my way back to that room. That room filled with love and meaning and work and creativity and awe and beauty. It's the room that I intend to live in for as long as I can. When I can't I intend to visit it often to marvel at its treasures and handle those pieces that so transformed and transfixed me. And when I can no longer manipulate the artifacts of my specific humanity anymore, I intend to nest in them once more as I did the first time, in order to feel that pride and love and warmth until I die, smiling at what was and what is.

This document is a map of sorts to a memory or two. An artist's description of the work in real time to be used by me as a patron of the museum in the future. It will help me access more fully the pieces that are before me. I'm compelled to do this to make up for all those pieces I didn't log in this way due to exhaustion and the foolish belief that the memories would be so powerful as to never drift away into the ether. Perhaps I thought them permanent in some way, a way that would make documenting it formally a waste of time. Foolish indeed and I should have known better. But, ours is not to wonder why, and so forth...

What follows is for you, yes, reader, truly it is. Knowing that you read, and that you are occasionally moved to engage with me has also added immensely to my experience. But it is also for me and for my wife and our kids. A log of sorts, though I hope an artful one, capturing this time. A fool's errand to be sure, and likely a fruitless and hopelessly failing attempt to capture just a piece of its essence for our future enjoyment.

Teddy sits in my lap, every night sometime between 8 and 8:30, bathed and brushed and comfy in his pajamas. He's my little bedtime buddy. He'll cry when I pick him up and momma gives him his Elmo doll. A doll too small to be his lovey, but it is what he has chosen and our many attempts to provide him with a larger, more plush and easier-to-find-in-your-sleep or in the darkness of waking at 2AM doll have been shunned. 'Mo-Mo', as he calls him, is his guy. The rest are discarded, literally thrown overboard, if he notices them. Two dolls other than Mo-Mo stay in the bed, a floppy brown bunny and a standard issue bear, but they are so untouched as to be unnoticed. The routines are a dead giveaway now and he cries and lunges for mommy when it clicks for him that it is bedtime. She is a bit more pliable in terms of keeping to the schedule in general and he thinks if he could just get me to hand him over to her, he'd be able to avoid his fate. Neither momma nor I pay any attention to this complaint anymore as it ceases by the time we get to the stairs, a walk of no more than 12-15 adult steps from anywhere on the first floor of our small and perfect little suburban home, and usually not more than 5 steps from where he's been picked up, in the living room.

Once to the stairs we make a dramatic flourish of thrusting our hands upward, toward the second floor, a show of bravado that he and I enjoy and one that always brings a smile to his face. Thusly we proceed up the stairs, following our outstretched hands and giggling when we get to the top. The theatricality of it all is just plain silly, but if you haven't seen him do it it's just not altogether possible to understand how adorable it is. He is not going to have these cheeks, these bubbly, adorable cheeks, for much longer, but for the time being anything I can do to make him smile, I will.

Once on the landing we turn left to the bedrooms. Theirs one to the right, but we loaded up all our stuff in it when we moved in and now only reference it if something is in there which needs to be extracted or if we need a place to shove things when people are coming over. It is now, and

I imagine will forever be referred to by Karen and I as 'the cottage'. We christened it when it became the place we flopped down in when we'd pushed enough crap to the sides to lay out a futon mattress and it became the place where sick parents slept, or where we'd lie during that glorious long weekend when we had managed to get them napping at the same time. Our room shared a wall with theirs and we weren't going to risk even the possibility of being the reason they might wake up.) I plop him down and he runs into his room. Once there he looks around for a second spots the glider chair that was initially used for nursing but is now the rocking chair, and makes a break for it. I pretend to be outraged and shocked, every night, that he's going to sit in daddy's chair, and he struggles his way up there, climbing like a pro, sits proudly and takes in my displays of shock, both facial and audible, and laughs proudly. I don't know if you have access to a two year old, but if you do, spend AS MUCH TIME AS POSSIBLE watching them walk around in pajamas. It's just awesomely cute. Then I pick him up, turn on various, strategically placed little lights, turn off others, turn on a bit of white noise and proceed to work my way through his stack of books until he decides he's done, or we finish all of them. To this point, we've only added and not yet removed any of his books. Little Blue Truck and Goodnight Gorilla are the musts but usually it's all of them. I've dozed off while reading. One of the pleasant side effects of this phase of life for me is that I have no trouble falling asleep. It's getting to be a lot. I always roust quickly enough, but his weight and warmth on my lap, the dim lights and the repetitive pleasantness of the books have a mildly narcotic effect on me. Once done I sing to him. Usually starting with Twinkle Twinkle Little Star, then You Are My Sunshine... I may hum from there, I may move to the Beatles. Some Blackbird, some early parts of Hey Jude, maybe some God Only Knows by the Beach Boys. I usually put him down at this time, but yesterday he made me hold him for a bit and kept bringing my hand up to his cheek, so it rested on him, fully holding his face on the outside, while the inside was pressed against my chest while he sat in my lap. If a meaning of life can be said to be a visceral feeling rather than a thought or a defined purpose, this is one of the meanings of my life.

This is one of the routines that evolve early in life that feel like they will last forever, but tend to last a few weeks to a few months before necessity forces them to change or the child simply loses interest and the routine is no longer effective. While I haven't done a wonderful job of logging them, as I'm doing now, I hope to do more in the near future. Hopefully this is a nostalgic dad's lament, chapter 1. I want to go back to the old video's and photos and jog memories and come back here and record them in detail, as much detail as possible, before they are all gone and I look at the photos and see my beautiful boy and remember everything he ever said, but start saying things like, 'I don't remember that apartment so much anymore. Was Charlie born yet when we moved in there? Was he only in the apartment for the first year or was it closer to two?'

I don't want that fate. But it or some more addled version of that state, or some less benevolent version of it is surely approaching. Just as new and exciting and enriching phases of my kids' lives are heading this way. So rather I log my memories, in pictures and in words in hopes that those triggers will trigger in me responses that will transport me in an instant back to that dark room, in our still disheveled, not fully occupied or appointed tiny little house where I can giggle with Charlie over the silliness of him pretending to be a dog named Sonny. Where I can pretend his carrots are puppy treats, a move I've stolen from his mother, in a multipurpose front room with makeshift changing stations and an unused fireplace and gates blocking every exit. To the place where my little boy won't let me take my hand from his cheek. Where he will simply find the hand if it goes missing, and place it back on his cheek as he knows that is what's needed. He's right, and it's one of the chief pleasures of my entire existence, and I will become a silly nostalgist adrift in gauzy memories and I will lose all currency and relevancy willingly if it will help me to remember this beautiful place of messy, sloppy, crazy love where our family began.

7 Lessons Learned While Learning OnThe Job... A Dad's Notes

I'm pretty new to this endeavor. My kids are 2 and 3, both boys. My wife and I are very happy with how things are progressing, but like everyone who finds themselves in this predicament, we have found there's an endless supply of new challenges to be conquered. At different times we could really have used a more experienced parent's advice. But where to turn? Simply no one has any advice for parents! Crazy, right? Thought I'd give away freely some knowledge that I've managed to learn over time. Some of it was evident and obvious and surely something anyone could figure out, and some of it was only stumbled upon, accidentally, in the dark after thinking the situation hopeless. Regardless, I hope you can benefit from whatever it is I've learned.

1. The Great Illusion: The Dr.'s will tell you that your child needs an incredible, seemingly unattainable number of hours of sleep per day. As babies it's like 15+ and through toddler years it's still close to 12. Yet this is countered by the many parents in your life that will tell you how tired they are and how much their kid has ended sleep for them. What I found was that my kid was within range of all the targets the Dr.'s set forth but I only discovered this if I'd track the hours. Left to my intuitive reckoning on those days my baby slept 15+ hours it never felt like it. Which is inscrutable? How can someone sleep in excess of 60% of the day, yet still manage to have that sleep be at such inconvenient times for the sleep cycles of their adult? It's baffling.

2. TV is an excellent babysitter: I'm in no way saying that you can go out to dinner or leave them unattended. I'm simply saying that set to the right programs, with ample food and liquids available and fresh diapering applied its remarkable how refreshing it can be for anywhere from 20 mins to an entire afternoon to know they are fine, fed and safe. Sure, I'd prefer they were being read to, but they will be. Later. And it will be the same six board books that you will read to them interminably. So give yourself a break, set up some Curious George or Team UmiZoomi and check your Facebook feed. You deserve it.

3. Kids will sleep wherever and whenever they choose to: So make bedtime whatever the hell you want it to be. If you want them never to feel the sting of being removed from your room then put them in their own room night one and be happy with your choice. Or put them in your bed and let nature decide when they are to leave. Use a co-sleeper or don't. Cuddle them to bed or sing and pat their back. Let them cry it out or pick them up whenever you hear a noise or the urge hits. Whatever you wanna do, do that. Because you're the grown up and it's not only about what's best for them in vacuum, it's about what's best for the collective you. In our experience getting the first one out of our bedroom happened at 6 months or so, and he was never in the bed. For the second it went closer to a year because it was our last go around and we wanted more of it. He's also found his way to our bed from time to time. No biggie. Both have worked, and worked is a malleable term. So have at it.

4. Children have evolved to survive our ineptitude: It is an elegant system that has come to be. They are adorably cute and perfectly designed to cause in us a worry we have never experienced before, driven mostly by love and also mostly by fear. Love of this perfect creature, flawless in every way, sure to bring great joy to a world it has been sent to brighten. Fear that this perfect specimen has been mistakenly left in your wildly inept and uninformed hands and the wellbeing of all mankind hangs perilously in the balance. Its crazy intense and it's no time for perspective. You believe it is the end all and be all. And you need to. How else would you have the energy?

No kidding, when we brought our first home we stayed awake, one of us at all times, to watch him sleep and make sure he didn't stop breathing. It was crazy dumb, and because we're who we are and he was who he was, entirely unavoidable. But the reality is he was in the perfect position to survive us and our crushing stupidity. Emerging competent takes months, years even, and feeling competent still isn't a definite, at least not for us. So it's wonderful that as we navigate all this learning, and tolerate the incredible strain a baby has on you personally and the wear it can have on your relationship during those early years, we get to navigate it in a space that is hyper real for us, like the most intensely real moments of our lives and he won't remember or really be affected by any of it. It's gotten easier already. Things will get harder again, but that early time is bananas. At least it was for us. But eventually we took a breath and realized we were doing this thing. It's a good feeling at the end of a long series of what feel like monumental screw-ups but is really just the normal learning curve for new parents.

5. Your home won't be fully clean and orderly for the foreseeable future: You'll make it nice for when relatives come over. At least at first. You'll learn how to create the illusion of neatness and order for the sake of society, but even that illusion will be difficult to reach and will ONLY be done so for guests. Again, you may be different, just want you to know that this is a real thing and if you fall into it, don't worry. It's just like that. For us we're getting close to a time when we might be able to host pizza Fridays for cousins on a regular basis soon. But we're four years in. And the sink is still full. So are the counters. I think a box of Cinnamon life lived between the fridge and the wall for over a year.

6. Dates can be had right at your kitchen table: Dating now is a frame of mind, not a set of plans and a reservation. Those opportunities to get out as grownups come so rarely that is hard to be assured you'll even be able to relax those shoulders on that specific night. So much of our wellbeing is now intermingled with our kids that we can't know when will be the right time for us to hang out like adults. The white noise and real noise of two toddler boys can really impinge on that. So if it doesn't happen the way you hoped it would on that rare, and in our case that means one single evening in the nearly four years we've had kids, night that you can get dressed and go out like grownups, don't sweat it... wait for that time you're making each other laugh during evening clean up and pounce. Break out the wine and beer, set up a space free of kid flotsam and jetsam and have at it. Dating is now a thing to be captured in the wild rather than planted and cultivated like it was before. Feeling flirty and fun and attracted to your spouse in any way, ride that wave as far as it will take you!

7. There is a new found understanding and empathy on your part for parents you might have judged before you knew: It's true. You can't know what it is a parent is talking about until you've been there. Parenting is very much like magic mushrooms this way. At least that's what I'm told. I remember being in your shoes and having strong opinions about parenting practices and about specific parents in particular. As a camp director and behaviorist I may have been the judgiest of all. But going through it is very democratizing. It breaks you fully down, but it then rebuilds you, modifying you for what your life will be now. This has compelled me to feel for those experiencing it for the first time especially, but for all parents in general as well. It makes you root for them. You know it's touch and go their early on for everyone. Emotions and hormones run high while sleep and patience run low. So feel for the brothers and sisters going through it. Support those looking like they've given up. Let them know you've been there. Remind them about the benefits of TV's and Ipads, and NEVER tell them something they are happy with is WRONG. Who the f**k do you think you are? If it provides them any comfort just shut up, be happy for them and share your judgements of others with your spouse at the aforementioned kitchen table dates. Otherwise, keep that mess to yourself and put forth only love, understanding and acceptance. It's my experience that despite many mistakes and many more to come, and short of total incompetence the likes of which are highly unlikely in anyone reading this, nothing you can do, as long as you love them and are doing the best you can, will really hurt them in the long run. Try your damnedest to identify with the mom who's kid is going ape in the hall and being a total bratty 4 year old and know that you are them and they are you. It's an interesting thing to feel an instant connection, a deep and abiding one, with strangers who are enjoying this most primal and connective experience we are able to have as humans. I for one relish it.

Our Second First Date

It's strange to sit across from a person you clearly love, you're clearly committed to and realize that you've forgotten how to be alone with them. I mean how can you be uncomfortable with a person with whom you have an open-door bathroom policy. With whom you are in the midst of a nearly decade long conversation.

I'll tell you how. Have kids and don't even pretend to take care of yourself. Fall so head over heels in love with your kids and be so bowled over and unprepared emotionally that without a word you both decide to fling off all sense of reason and balance and dive headfirst into losing yourself in your kids. It's exactly as unhealthy as it sounds. We made not even a passing attempt at fooling ourselves. We were goners at first sight. The last time we were on a date, one with drinks and hopes of romance, we were entirely different people. Our lives have been taken over by kids and we gave up our other identities long ago.

So when it finally came around, last weekend, our first true date in four years, we were woefully unprepared to let the shoulders down. We'd captured romance in the wild from time to time in the years since and we are as solid as solid can be. She is the love of my life and I'm perfectly comfortable stating that I'm the love of her life. But there is no sense denying that the giant elephant that trampled our previous selves has left us with some work to do.

We found ourselves across from one another in a quiet restaurant chosen by our former selves. Two people full of ideas and interests eagerly and enthusiastically looking to share and listen to this person we wanted to impress. Those people while still in their same shells, sort of, were gone. All we could think of was the kids. We both wanted this to be about something else, but what else is there at this point? They aren't only our beloved children, they're also our only context for a relationship at this point. It was uncomfortable. They didn't even serve alcohol so we couldn't loosen up chemically to hope to spark things. Nope. Just blank stares, apologies for everything, unable to get out of each other's way. It was awkward and painful. In fact, by the time they came for the order we had already decided to get a RIDICULOUSLY overpriced appetizer each, to woof it down and get out of their as soon as possible. Which is exactly what we did.

We moved on to a pub. Sports on the TV's, loud music and 50 or so adventurous and ordinary beers on tap. It was the best thing we could have done. We both started to unwind and we removed the unwritten rule that we had imposed about not talking about the kids. We ordered french fries and onion rings and about a beer in our shoulders relaxed and we started delighting in making one another laugh. Some of the laughter was about the kids, some of it was about our own foibles. Some of it was about what was occurring in the room. In the moment. It was a delight. It was natural and easy. Before long we were up to our old tricks. I may have even convinced her to write a guest post as 'Developing Mom'. We welled up and we cracked up and we felt a giant spark and shared excitement. We started to plan our future dating life now that we had a wonderful babysitter (a story for another time). We made sure to have enough cash to tip her graciously so as to be sure she'd be willing to come back. Two toddlers isn't every 25 year olds idea of an awesome Saturday night. Then we started to cop to our general difficulty. Its midwinter and the combination of cabin fever, short days and freezing cold had made us both hard to be around from time to time. Not to mention the daily challenges of raising the boys. We haven't always been either fair or loving to one another and it did us both some good both to admit it, and to be relieved of some of the responsibility for it by the other helping to carry the load.

I'm getting excited. We learned some things on our second first date. We certainly have more things to learn going forward. But what's becoming clear to me and I think to us, is that we have to do some work on our own at this point. Each of us on our own have to think about how we want to engage the world around us and who we are each going to be as we slowly get out from under the crushing awesomeness of new parenthood. We have to share our new ideas and new dreams of the future with one another as many of the parameters have changed in the years since we related to each other what those dreams originally were. We have to discover ourselves again. We get to discover each other again.

I fell in love with my wife almost instantly when we met. We were married a year and a half later and we were parents 2 years after that. What's happened since has changed us and we have to take time to remember those people that we were. The wonderful thing is that I get to do it all over again. At this stage of the game there's nothing that holds so much excitement as getting the chance to fall in love all over again with the woman I love more than anything.

Facebook, Parenthood and the Bursting of the Bubble

Parenting is isolating. Kids make you a recluse. Many of us find our way to Facebook. From what I'm told Facebook has gone the way of the dinosaur insofar as social media is concerned. This is fine with me. Gets rid of all the youthful riff-raff and their unintelligible slang. Seriously. I'm far more comfortable with outdated technology as long as I'm rarely asked to change and can avoid being constantly reminded of my impending irrelevancy. Anyway, Facebook is where grownups, people of a certain age can see and be seen. It's a place to brag and to bitch. And to bitch and to bitch and to bitch. It's a place where, if you construct your network right, you can find endless support and understanding from peers in the same boat not to mention a good deal of criticism and snark. Some warranted, mostly just the rantings of similarly frustrated people enjoying the most wonderful, treacherous days of their lives, looking to act out.

As one ages and creeps toward ultimate decrepitude one becomes wistful for times past. Times that our psyches have ably transformed from the real life reality they were into a magical utopia of proper thinking and moral rightness. I find myself judging things that are new (in this case meaning things my parents didn't do or have, be they normative parenting expectations or technological doodads) to be lacking in a certain moral fiber that allows me to judge them righteously rather than responsibly. This is the 'young whippersnapper' maneuver, and I'm growing quite enamored of it.

We have lost something valuable by not ever losing touch with our peer groups. Their used to be a natural incubation period after having kids that we've lost due to constant interconnectedness. Someday we'll evolve to intuitively know how to handle being in front of everyone we know and having a front row seat while they stand before us. We'll know how to consume the media in an intelligent way that allows us to know the tricks that both our friends and our minds are playing on us. But that won't be me. For now, for me, there's something lost by not becoming a hermit for a decade or so after you have kids. It's the way nature and my environment trained me to navigate such a traumatic and magical transformation.

In the past we all had kids. Over time the acceptable ages for this (attention-seeking) behavior has crept ever upward. Until now, when I'm engaged in the absurd task of caring for toddlers in my 40's. Seriously. This is where I have failed nature. This isn't the way this is supposed to be done. One by one, or occasionally two by two, we all split from our various friend/social groups. Facebook is a help this way as I can remain a voyeur on my former mates, but the truth is I don't stay in touch. It's an aspect of my character. I used to think it a flaw, but it's not, it's just who I am. Having this window into my former lives is hugely valuable. It's also somewhat detrimental. You see, I was meant to go into a bubble, hermetically sealed from the eyes of others, for years. I was meant to do so in order to fully allow me the time to transform into a standard issue dad, delighting in the originality of my bad puns and relishing the comfort of my ever diminishing fashionability. A sense that in my case was formed in the era of skater/grunge/B-Boy styles that has thankfully left my formerly clownishly oversized clothing nearly perfectly fitted now that I've 'grown' into manhood. Furthermore the bubble is a place populated by your parents and siblings and neighbors with similarly aged kids and it was here where you learned what you were supposed to be like. Not anymore. Now we hide from our neighbors, hang on desperately to our classmates and original peer groups and never allow ourselves the period where we are supposed to fully forget how we are viewed by anyone other than our kids and our spouses and our larger family. That blessed bubble has been burst.

In the bubble your non-parent friends took on the same feeling of irrelevancy to you as you did to them. You knew something they didn't and you knew you couldn't 'tell' them anything you'd learned. They had to find it for themselves. And you went about grocery shopping and eating dinners at home and raising kids and building a foundation and ensuring healthcare and playing chauffeur and doing laundry, good god the laundry, and midnight feedings and 4AM cuddles and reading books a thousand times and living like children yourselves eating recooled leftover chicken nuggets and half apple sauces 4 nights a week and turning every available floor into a play area and generally living in a home too messy, though thoroughly sterilized, to ever host friends and barely passable to host family. You know, doing the day to day stuff that would allow your kids to go out and one day have the same disregard for their friends once they had kids because it's the circle of life.

In the process you grew to care less and less about what others thought and started to anchor your life around your couch, kitchen and your place of employment. You lost touch with culture and one day realized you hadn't seen any of the movies nominated in five years, but you know every word to every Pixar or even Pixar-ish film that's ever been made and you like it that way. Whole presidential campaigns and fashion trends would pass without your notice and you'd find yourself thinking of a night out to The Macaroni Grille as a treat. It would go like this. For years. Decades even.

You'd also get to navigate boyhood again, making many of the same mistakes, but fixing some and taking pride in the fact that those things you avoided the second time around were out of the lineage and wouldn't even be issues for your grandkids. And in the process, the person you were helming this seemingly out of control ship with was that beautiful girl you couldn't believe liked you all those years ago and you are now family with her, the only immediate family you'll ever have who was totally chosen, picked out special, and you are in more than love with her. You're in LIFE with her. With her alone. She's the only one that gets it. Gets it the exact same way as you do. And you are in love again, but a better kind. A more complete kind. You've done all the work together and you've beaten out any of the doubt or concern and are fully yourself and made to feel great about yourself, your fatter, less relevant, but fully realized self.

There was something nice about a world where we simply retreated to build a safe bubble for our kids to grow up in and ourselves to grow unselfconscious in. Where the world was not dominated by competitive parenting. Where we befriended other families at the park and on the street and they became our family friends. Where our only advice came from our own parents and siblings and not the 'new parent industrial complex' out to capitalize on our natural feelings of inadequacy, out to exacerbate and exploit them so we'd buy and buy again their book, their foods, their methods and anything else they can charge us for. A place you could emerge from culturally irrelevant and personally powerful. Clad in polyester pants with a too high waist looking the embarrassment you are to your now prepubescent kids, proudly out of fashion and unfit. Providing them a model of the 'truly cool' person who cares not what the world wants them to be but rather places value on that which is truly important in seeking and finding lasting happiness. Forget having good self-esteem. You were past that. You knew who you were and what that meant. You were a parent.

But you whippersnappers with your fancy 'thinking machines' and the Facebook have gone and ruined it.

Bah..

The Hum

We occasionally find ourselves dissatisfied with life. Not unhappy, just, blah. Suddenly, without warning, we feel like we are failing. Our whole lives are on display and in the way all the time.

We have a small kitchen area that has been blocked by gates since moving in over two years ago. The dumping ground it has become makes us feel bad. As has the general disarray of our modest home tasked with holding the detritus of a life being lived by two toddlers and two parents that both work full time. The fridge is a mess. There is a general paper explosion starting in a basket on our counter that bursts forth slowly, perpetually until it occupies half our free counter space, at which point we just plow them back until they so overwhelm us that we take a day off to organize them, starting the process over. There's been an empty bottle of olive oil on the counter for weeks, months perhaps. The bags that sit inside the gate reach out into the room and are scattered between the edge of the kitchen and the door leading to the garage (not to mention the disaster that is the garage) and are so permanent that any topographical map of our little kitchen would have to include them as permanent features. The TV's on. The monitor's on. Every godforsaken screen is covered in dirty, sticky toddler finger prints and I daren't guess what lurks in the back of the cabinets. The top of the fridge. The top of the damned fridge.

Adding to this is the general unwellness of parenthood. It's true. Your spirit soars with the magic of new life, new life designed to inspire your heart to give up on all self-care in order to bathe this child with love and affection and the endless hours of work it takes to present them clean and fed and rested to the world. Leaving you generally speaking about 36 hours from a shower in either direction at all times. This defies all logic, but is so. You're left with back pain from the terrible posture required of you nearly constantly. You are fat from a diet of kid's foods often, healthy grown up foods rarely and downing copious amounts of coffee just to live. The kind of coffee binging that leaves you so dehydrated that it hurts to pee and you say things like, 'man, I really need to start drinking some water', while you sip another coffee, pour the water, only to find it the following weekend in the very place you've been looking past it since you put it down. A week ago. Full.

Then there is the noise that keeps you a bit crazy these days. Exhaustion has a sound, and it sounds like whining to everyone in ways you find embarrassing way too late, about how tired you are. You are a cliché, and that hurts when you're aware enough to notice it. But how could you when you are so distracted by your obsession with avoiding mirrors. I mean, you look grey. There, I said it. I'm fat and grey and I don't know if I'll ever bounce back. To cope with this I choose candy. Lots of it. So what. The only people I'm starring for are my kids these days. Well the lady of the house too, but she's in this with me.

Then there's the noise. My children's voices and the things they say take my breath away dozens of times a day. They are magical, truly special creatures and I assume my honesty on this blog I write is about the only thing that can keep each of them from being re-elected as President of the United States. But I seriously wouldn't be surprised if they overcame that too. They're that amazing. But the reality of each day is that your toddler can be amazing 36-48 times a day and still leave you with hours upon hours of really challenging behavior. Challenging behavior that comes with tears and maniacal comic-book-villain laughs and screams just to scream, just to startle you into looking, only to find a giant ear to ear grin on this little boy that just screamed like he was being stretched by Prince Humperdinck's henchman. All to the soothing sounds of the most infernal and dastardly aural creation the world has ever known: The Fresh Beat Band. Actually we haven't really watched them in a couple years, but I still hear them. Everywhere.

The mess. The exhaustion. The noise. The work. This hum that so annoys me each day. This hum that I can't stand at times. This hum that causes my wife and I to lose patience with each other far more often then we'd care to admit. This hum that we so desperately wish to quiet will one day fully dissolve. Already the nights are longer, and the boys are bigger and if pressed I can become sentimental about 3 AM wake up calls for feeding and the tiny fingers that looked like a dolls.

The thing about this hum, this hum that I have a really hard time embracing and complain about far more than I ought to is that it will someday disappear. The corners will be clean, as will the counters and the floors. The TV will be on to entertain only us and the noise of a full house will dissipate and be replaced by more pleasant and welcome noises. We will be allowed to enjoy silence, sweet sweet silence. The exhaustion won't ever fully go, but it will get more manageable. The hum will fade, like all other things, to history. When it does I suspect I will relish the clean and the quiet. It will allow me all the free time I'll need to look back and appreciate all that was done here. To appreciate the times I couldn't appreciate fully in the moment. To fully embrace and love the hum that I'll never get the privilege to be enveloped in ever again.

An Optimists View of Death and Life

The math is simple. It takes a metric ton of everyday magic to equal an ounce of disappointment. And if you are tired of looking for the magic in the everyday it starts to disappear. It turns invisible. If you aren't careful the equation will flip and you'll find yourself living in a world of everyday disappointment struggling to see even an ounce of magic.

It's a well-trodden path for men and one I find myself at the precipice of, trying to avoid it. We've all seen men whose faces have twisted into joylessness. Worse, after a time the mask becomes one of distaste, as if a terrible, acrid smell is coming from their own lip, unavoidable and constant. I can see how they get there from here. The reality is that if you choose to view life as linear and finite it's heading to a destination that is lamentable. Particularly if you avoid the magic. After all the darks greatest virtue is patience.

I'm 41 years old. I'm no longer free to think of old age as something I may be able to avoid. It's a magical thought of youth. Sure, there are many for whom it's a more pressing matter, but the truth is that I have an understanding from this vantage point that I didn't have as a younger man. Things I long for more than anything are gone forever and I'm going to die. I'm going to die. All of this is going to end. None of this is permanent. My time on earth, even if it's longer than my fair share, even if it's longer than anyone's ever, is but a blip. It is not a thing, my conscience, which is inherent. It's in fact fleeting and ultimately temporal. It's true for me and for you and whether we think about it or not, we know it. In our bones we know it.

I'm gonna die and the things I didn't recognize as wonderful in life, that I didn't wallow in, aren't coming back. What's worse, I can no longer go forth in the blissful ignorance of youthful disbelief. We are funny animals that can know a thing and perceive such fault in it that we can convince ourselves that the truth doesn't pertain to us. There comes a time when we have to process this information.

My greatest fear when confronting this reality is that I will become so angry that I'll lose the life left in me rather than use it all up for every minute I'm afforded it. I see it in the men that have come before me. Not my father or even my lineage, but in life. It's an old trope, the idea of the grumpy old man. In many ways it's how the world would prefer for us to go, for sure. Anger is quite self-reliant and needs little from the world other than reason, and the world can give anyone with anger reason. Far too many men jump on that reason and ride it comfortably to death. It's a way to go. I'm very happy to discover it isn't my way to go.

I'm able to hold death at bay by befriending it. It's taken on a large role in my life since having kids. I'm less concerned by others concerns if I remind myself I'm going to die. I'm going to have to do very hard things and death is going to be a constant in my life from this point forward to be sure. Truth is death is always all around you, always was and always will be. The forces of optimism and pessimism are at war both within me and without me. But once I accept my fate and digest that death is a part of life it's up to me to recognize which side I'm on. Truth is optimism and joy are the only right answer for me.

I happen to think this is it. If there's such a thing as heaven I believe I'm a happy resident of it now. This place demands much of me, but it's given far more than it's taken. Truth is it will be up to those left to provide the memory of my life with meaning. I'm pretty happy with that arrangement. Besides, I've got plenty of time left to still discover who I can become. Freed of the burden of fighting against what's to come, the curiosity is adding life to these years...

I have no special shield protecting me from getting angry in old age. It's a face you see on so many men. Twisted in thought or distaste. But there is a trick. It's a practice not an outlook. It's called gratitude.

I'm so incredibly thankful for all I've been afforded. Everything from the air I breathe to the family I was made by to the amazing time of miraculous ingenuity in which I will have spent my life. I'm thankful for the understanding and forgiveness that's been shown to me. By the love that's been heaped upon me and received so graciously by those I've been so lucky to know. I'm grateful for the confusion and the challenges that have pushed me to understand more than I otherwise would have. I'm even thankful for the tragedies that have taken place, for they have never failed to ignite compassion and love and humanity.

I'm thankful to for my life; for the memories that are mine and mine alone. I'm thankful that we are all given this gift. I'm thankful that no matter how many people come and go during my time here, no matter how many people come and go through all of time, mine will have been the one and only experience that was this one. And I've been given a brain and senses that can recreate so many times from my life by simply choosing to close my eyes and conjure. I'm glad that forces beneath and above my control can cause so many wonderful and warm memories of this magical life to sneak up on me and arrest me on the spot and return me to the most blissful times of my life. Times I may not have been able to appreciate as they were occurring are waiting for the right moment, for the moment when I'm ready to appreciate them. I'm thankful for the people and the feelings and the time and joy.

How We Found Out Our Kid Had Food Allergies

I've heard that there's no style of learning more effective than experiential learning. This stands to reason. I have some experience in this area. Here are some things I've thought and some things I've learned.

I've thought, 'What a freaking nuisance. You know this is just an overprotective helicopter mom and because of her, because of these two or three nut jobs I can't make myself a damn peanut butter sandwich without breaking building ordinances. Anywhere.'

I've thought, 'Don't worry about it. We've got it covered. Sure, little Billy's mama made a stink about it, but we got one of the pizza's with soy cheese. We're not jerks, of course we want the kid to be safe and able to have fun.'

I've thought, 'This is mom's issue. The poor kid gets stuck at the table with all the other kids he doesn't know and has to have a special plate of crap brought out to him with his name on it. All because mom loves the attention she gets calling 13 times a day to make sure he's not eating anything other than what is on the stupid list.'

I've thought, 'Seriously, what's the worst that could happen?'

I've rolled my eyes and used air quotes when explaining that a kid in my care, but not my kid, had 'food allergies' and gone on to explain in coded but withering judgment of said child's mom and her hyper anxiety.

Whether it was coincidence or not it was always the moms.

Thank god, none of these misconceptions had fatal outcomes or even critical ones.

Then experience came knocking and taught me in an afternoon how mistaken I was.

Do you remember your 9/11 story? I do. For years after that terrible day anytime you were with someone you either didn't know before or hadn't seen since before that day the conversation always got around to your story. Your experience of that day. Still happens, just not as much as more and more 'adults' are not of an age to have remembered it or you're so familiar with everyone's tales that you reference rather than recount them.

Well, parents of kids with anaphylactic food allergies engage in the telling and retelling of their tale whenever we find someone that gets it. Unfortunately for us and our kids, parents of kids with anaphylactic food allergies are the only ones that get it. Each of us encounters the 'me' from above who doesn't get it and we know they don't get it and it can only make us act crazier. See we have to be crazy, insane. So crazy that you'd rather just bitch about me and my hyper anxiety then have to deal with my crazy wrath if any of my seemingly bizarre and self-centered requests are found to have been ignored. We've been granted the greatest education possible through our experiences. Here's what I've learned.

Many parents have a crazy period early in their first child's life, first week or two, when they can't stop thinking that it's possible that the baby will stop breathing and just die. We had this bit of experiential learning ourselves and for a 10 day period after getting the kid home one of us was awake at all hours of the day and night to make sure this didn't happen. How we'd stop it if it did is something we never even considered. Just seemed the right thing to do. Then you realize, this is crazy, if he's gonna give us a few minutes we need to take them. You learn these fears are baseless.

Then, a year later or so, we were having our normal lunch. Then little red pin pricks around his red and watering eyes. That's weird. Then bright red blotches all over his face and a high whistle of air trying to get in and out. Then running to the car. Then heavy vomiting as it's the only way it seems to breathe. Then, no breathing and beat red.

Then enormous vomiting. Here's something. Do you know where you park at the ER if your baby of 1 year of age is red and unable to breathe, turning purple and all of you and your wife and your baby are covered in vomit as he writhes to try to loosen the vice grip of the snake he feels choking him, only it's not a snake, it's his own body choking him from the inside? Where ever the f**k you want. In our case it was at the door. The car was vomit filled, and I mean covering the windows, all of them, including the windshield. By at the door, I mean they see you and guide you right to the door. You leave your car there running, doors open.

I don't know about you, but my experience at the ER has never failed to include a stop for at least a second of triage. Not us. They see a baby, see he's barely holding on to his precious little life and the breaths are gone, they point and TELL you, 'RUN!!' and you do. Your adrenaline is flooding your body and brain and you do it. You run.

When you get there you don't care who it is. You just need someone to save your baby's life. They do. You calm down on the outside and panic on the inside as you help your baby calm down. Eventually he's laughing and playing and you and your wife are trying to reflect his carefree demeanor, sneaking in conversation about what the hell could it be. You won't get answers until you see the allergist in a few days. So you empty your kitchen.

Almost all of it. Because something in there can cause that silly fear you had as new parents to be a reality. Your little love can just die. Its knowledge you carry until there is either a cure or you die. That's it. That's the list of all the ways you'll come to stop worrying. You get better at living with the knowledge, but you reorder everything. Used to have a career working in the city, but since I know from all my conversations how many people think this whole 'food allergy thing' is being way overblown by nervous parents, I pretty much ignore that job and rest on the laurels I'd earned and after that on the sheer audacity to just show up late, leave early or not show up at all, while trying to find something that works closer to home, since you're told that if he goes into shock the staff at the daycare's can't go with him, he'll just be taken by the ambulance, terrified, waiting hours, hopefully, until we arrive. So, I take a 20,000 pay cut and take a gig, a good gig, one I love, but a step down to be sure, to be with him for the day, feet away, always ready to run. Which you've done once and hope to never do again.

These experiences stick with you. Forever.

Burning Questions: Nick Jr. Edition

Sometime between the age of 3 months and a year the sights and sounds of kid's television become the droning background of many a parent's existence. At some point it's just inconsiderate to keep HGTV or ESPN on so we can ignore our little ones so we turn on one of a few channels providing round the clock entertainment for kids of varying ages so they can turn the tables and ignore us for a while. If you feed them and powder them at some point you might even get two hours out of it. If you've read this far you are a parent. If you are a parent, especially one with little ones present or in your recent past, you know that a couple of hours is nothing short of 1980 Olympic Hockey team miraculous.

Before you know it you are humming maddeningly catchy theme songs in the few moments you have to yourself. Or at work, that miraculous place where you can get a coffee or take a leak without any logistical issues delaying either. What the hell. Why would I be humming the Wallykazam theme song here? The one damn place I can listen to my own music. DAMMIT!

Eventually you come to possess deep knowledge of the programs that have been forced into your brain in a clockwork orange fashion brainwashing. But at some point the 2 hour nights of sleep turn to 3 hour nights then to 4 and perhaps as much as 5. I don't know yet. We're still hovering around 4, but I don't want to give up hope that this might grow. As you regain and reclaim your humanity and your bodily function returns to a place of stasis you are able to fully acclimate to your new world. Once this occurs the wine on a Saturday night comes back, some grown up shows start appearing in the Netflix recommendations and before you know it, you're a grownup and a parent and you can think again. As a result, seemingly without any prompting you turn your long dormant critical and analytical brain toward this world that consumed you for so long. You have questions about what it is you've become an expert in. Television for babies and toddlers. The following are my questions as it relates to the programs on Nick Jr., a favorite in our house.

Max & Ruby

Where the hell are your parents?

I asked this question on my Facebook page for the blog and got more responses then I have for anything I've ever posted. Ever.

Also, what is the message being sent when you take the forever observant, thoughtful and prepared, if a bit bossy (though keep in mind, by all accounts she's a little girl bunny left to raise her brother, parentless) Ruby and have her always lose in the end to the ever defiant, never attentive, positively dangerous Max, who seems to have the Midas touch?

Blaze and the Monster Machines

You named yourself, 'Blaze'. The reference is lost on no one. How in god's name did you get the theme song, which repeatedly punctuates the heroic actions of anthropomorphic monster trucks past the suits at your company with the refrain of, 'Let's Blaze!'?

Paw Patrol

What kind of municipal budget must you have to have a single outfit for community service providing all manner of emergency first response completely staffed by dogs? I realize this is totally missing the point and a question that couldn't be asked by the target audience, but these are the things one thinks at some point. This is my life and these are my thoughts. Seriously.

Peppa Pig

What the hell is the deal with the constant fat shaming of Daddy Pig? I should note that it's possible this is tweaking some of my personal sensitivities as I'm coming to resemble my namesake.

The Fresh Beat Band

I loved you for 2 episodes. Now you inspire rage. No questions. Just a statement.

The Bubble Guppies

Why are you so insistent there be no logic, not even internal logic, in regard to the physics of your world? On a recent viewing there was a fire truck. You are under water! Worse, once they got to where they were going, they couldn't figure out how to get up high until they extended the ladder, which a fish then 'climbed' by SWIMMING UPWARDS NEXT TO IT!! I hate you.

Oswald

You were perfect. A little slice of Zen like heaven. Where did you go?

Mommy and Joey, XOXOXO

The most transformative moment of therapy for me didn't happen in a therapist's office, or even in therapy. It happened in a walk in closet that I'd made my writing room in the third floor walk-up in Astoria, where I lived. Truth is I was in therapy to be able to have this moment so I could move forward in my life and let go of the things I had been dragging around with me since childhood. It was in this small room, within a room, within my apartment surrounded by the thousands of written pages I'd been creating and hoarding for years in an attempt to understand who and why I was and am that I called my mother to tell her how she'd failed me.

I recounted things said without thinking that hurt. I recounted the things she said that were so confusing that I couldn't comprehend why she would share them with me as a kid. I recounted the times I'd felt alone and unfairly judged. I told her of feelings I'd been blaming her for decades. Literally decades. This wasn't as long ago as I wish it were. I told her things I'd latched onto and refused to let go of for eternity. I told her about feeling like I was ignored and left to raise myself. I told her about how angry I was at her and why.

I'm pretty good with words. Not to brag, but I have a pretty good vocabulary and the ability to take thoughts and convert them into succinct and coherent and downright concise sentences that cut to the heart of what I'm trying to say. At the beginning of our conversation I told her that I called to talk about the things that were between us. About our relationship because it had occurred to me that it was our relationship that was in fact sabotaging my ability to love and to feel loved. I unloaded on her the pile of blame that I could never get past. It was fairly brutal and brutally unfair. It was mean. Anyone listening would have said so. Anyone who wasn't my mother.

My mother is perhaps the toughest person anyone's ever met. She has bravely stared down a life I'll never have to. She's been processing horrible tragedies since her youth and finding evermore reason for joy and love. She is the strongest person I know. You have to be pretty close to see this and I was afforded a front row seat that night in my closet, crying to my mother at a makeshift desk, surrounded by endless papers containing a profound misunderstanding of what turns out was my very good fortune of being born to the family I now understand to be my greatest blessing.

I hit her with every unfair punch that night. I blindsided her. She took every single one of them and apologized.

For mistakes she'd made, for my pain, for misunderstandings that she couldn't have known were still hurting me until that moment. She apologized and said she loved me even when I'd blame her for things that I now see she couldn't have been a part of. When I called and started swinging wildly and emotionally she let her guard down and allowed me to punch away, telling me she was sorry, telling me I was brave for confronting her, telling me that I deserved better. It wasn't a lie. She meant it. Despite giving me EVERYTHING and being blamed for things that weren't hers to own she heard not an angry and aggressive and unfair man treating her poorly. She heard her son hurting. She heard her little boy screaming and crying that it wasn't fair. And she took it all. To make me feel better. She let me know that it was okay to blame her, even if it wasn't her fault, because she was mom and I would always be her boy.

I grew up fully in that moment. Seriously. I can tell you when I emotionally became fully a man and it was that night. I knew almost immediately upon expressing my pent up feelings that they had tricked me. Wisely. My feelings made me blame the one person strong enough to handle my impetuousness and bullying if I ever chose to unload it. The one person that could guide me to where I needed to go.

By the end of the conversation she was crying with me. She was telling me about her pain and letting me know I wasn't alone. Letting me know that I would always have someone who would understand. Her. Mom. She healed me that night. The cuts that bled at ten, the ones that mean everything to a kid, I had bandaged. Being a sensitive kid at heart, naturally the bleeding continued and instead of allowing these wounds to heal, instead of cleaning them and caring form them, I just kept applying more and more bandages every time the blood seeped through. Never healing, always covering up and hoping my cuts would one day stop bleeding through. But that's not how it works. You can't heal that way. You can only hide. That day my mother held my hand like I was a child and promised me that even though it might hurt, she was going to tear off my bandages and clean them up so I could heal properly. So I could put down the load I'd been carrying and move on.

I emerged from that conversation a changed and healed person ready to take on the next phase of my life. It was just in time as I was about to meet the woman that has since become a hero to both me and our sons. My mother gave me life, love and security and when I misplaced her gifts she dove into the hole I was drowning in and rescued me, despite my resistance.

I love you, mom. Thank you.

How My Wife Became a Poop Doula

Like riding a bike, I always presumed that pooping was one of those things that once you learned how to do it you pretty much had it down for the rest of your life. Turns out that journey is not so simple. Our four year old has apparently hit some bumps in the road. There are small, almost imperceptible changes occurring within me over time that might suggest there is the potential that this could be an issue for me as well, albeit in the distant future.

Anyway, there I was, sitting all smug up on the toilet catching up with my selected family and friends on my phone. This was my 'me' time. I didn't have to use the toilet, but it's a place a parent can sit on occasion, as long as one's spouse is there to occupy the kids, where they are given a moment's reprieve. I think of it as a panic room of sorts in the hour after dinner, before bedtime. A place to go to forget about life for upwards of 3 minutes. A spa. It was here that I came across and amusing post by my younger sister. I'm paraphrasing here, but it said something like, 'I'll NEVER get used to cleaning poop out of the tub!'. I responded the only way I knew how. 'Oh my god, that's so gross!'

After a minute or two, and after a few, more kindhearted friends and family expressed empathy and understanding in the comments, it occurred to me that I might be tempting fate. In an attempt at something of a reverse jinx I went back in to the comment thread and expressed something closer to thoughtfulness. Something like, 'Oh that so sucks. I'm so sorry. We've been lucky so far.' But I was totally faking it. That sh*t doesn't happen if you're careful and stay attenti...

'Joe! Oh no.. Joe!' My wife shouted from upstairs.

I was on the couch enjoying my own end of night screen time alongside the big boy, the four year old, the one in the clear from the possibility of such an accident when my life took a dark turn.

'T had an accident. In the tub!'

Oh crap.

I'm guessing that having made it this far through without this happening there are some parents that have made it all the way without dealing with this dark day. With the extracting by hand a turd that floats in parts and sinks in others like dynamited fish in a filthy pond. I remained calm on the outside because you need your children to know that although life is forever changed and we'll never be able to truly look each other in the eye again, that they are okay and that one must be strong in the face of fear. I am a role model.

Karma was not through with us.

Believing that we'd learned all we needed to learn in order to avoid this issue in the future, we let down our guard. Somehow a few days passed without our big boy making a poop family in the potty. That's what he calls it when it happens in phases. It's amazing what you find cute when your kids say it. When we pointed it out to him and asked him to try he was resistant in a way that only a four year old could be. He had become afraid to poop. We coaxed. We bribed. It worked a couple of times, but it hurt and came with tears. Then he just stopped. Refused. He would have intermittent bouts of pain due to his being backed up. We couldn't convince him with logic. We tried everything. What happens next is amongst the dumbest things I've ever done. I can't believe it occurred even as I sit here and write it. It's so dumb I'm embarrassed to say it. I decided that a good warm bath would do the trick. It did.

Our 4 year old is huge, like the size of a 7 year old. This is not an anecdote. He is the average size of a seven year old. I'll just say that it's possible for a backed up 4 year old, who is the size of a 7 year old to poop like a 41 year old who had a steak burrito and coffee for lunch. Through tears and the splashing of fecal infested dirty bath water we learned the power of karma and at that moment I knew it was done. Karma had made sure that I learned my lesson.

We are a modern family and my duties as a man are far more involved than men of previous generations. I am a competent and caring nurturer. Still, there are certain tasks that only a mother can perform. One of those tasks is exercised now when we note it's been a couple of days. Our elaborate system of rewards for willing poops (chocolate, funnily enough) is pretty good. But if we let it slide the fear returns. When it does my wife becomes the guide for our boy that he needs at that moment. They will retreat to the bathroom where she will allay his fears, stick with him through his vicious rebukes and tearful apologies, always reassuring him that this is how it has worked since the dawn of time. That despite his fears, he will live through this and be so happy with the results that he'll *choose willingly to do it again!* Eventually he believes her and they are one, holding hands as she provides him with the spiritual and emotional support allow his body to do what it's made to do.

Without intending to and being motivated only by deep deep love, my wife is now a poop doula.

7 Ways Having a Dog Totally PrepareYou for Parenthood

You skeptics. Seriously. You think that nobody without kids can understand how hard it is. That's just crazy. Sure, having kids, caring for them and raising them is a challenge. We all empathize. But you don't have to get so superior about it. I've even heard some people dismiss the attestations of pet-owners, dogs cared for since puppy-hood even, as not fully preparing one for the experience of having kids. Well, I say phooey to you. As skeptics I know what you need is evidence. Allow me to enumerate my argument.

1. **Love** - Until you've had a puppy, a precious baby dog, look up at you with those beautiful eyes expressing trust in you to care for her in ways that melt you, you can't know love. Plain and simple. The full weight of love is only felt with a puppy and can't be replicated by anything else. And as anyone who has seen a Nicholas Sparks movie adaptation knows, love is painful, guys. Seriously.

2. **Sleep** - I totally think this sleep thing that so many parents talk about is SO OVERDONE. It's a naked and frankly embarrassing cry for attention. As a

friend I try to be sure not to indulge it. It doesn't take a lot of looking to find out that science has shown that babies sleep like 15-18 hours a day. You want to talk about sleepless nights? Yeah. Has your kid ever chased down a porcupine and had quills stuck in its gums? No? Well, there we have it. You don't know sleeplessness my friend.

3. **Worry** - You parents act like the world isn't totally designed to help you. You wring your hands over your child in daycare all day. You know what you can do? You can call. You can ask a qualified professional how your child is doing. How your child who's been playing with friends and snacking on healthy food and being tended to at every turn, how they are as they nap peacefully. Not me. All I can do, ALL I CAN DO is worry.

4. **Cost** - Okay. I'll grant you college. But the likelihood of that out of control scam known as higher education being fixed by the time it's an issue for you is pretty good, so let's not overstate it here. Meanwhile, I have an animal that can need everything from mental health therapies (don't laugh, you have no idea how big a deal this is) and complex surgeries to prevent any number of ailments that are likely to compile and none of that is covered by any 'family' insurance plan. I mean

seriously, if this dog isn't family than I don't know what family is.

5. **Strain on Your Relationship** - Do you have any idea how hard a dog is to incorporate into your life. I mean really. It's like the hardest thing you can do. A baby, that's a strengthening of your bond, born of your shared DNA it can't help but bring you closer. Dogs are so SO needy. It's like you hardly even have time to spend with your significant other. In those early days, and we're talking easily 6 months here, I don't think we had our 'alone' time as a couple more than 4 or 5 times a week. What the hell is that? Babies don't do that, puppies do. Am I right!

6. **Potty Training** - I'm to understand this is unpleasant for you. Now imagine your baby naked and unable to wipe. At least unable to wipe without doing so with your carpet. I rest my case on this one.

7. **Guilt** - One word. Kennel.

I think I've made my point here. Don't be so sure I'm not ready to be responsible for a human life. To raise it and care for it. To love it and set it up for success and fend off the wolves at the gate. I've had a puppy, so I ain't scared!

12 Unflattering Headlines About Me as A Dad

1. Local 'Dad Blogger' Who Writes Often Of Commitment and Love Will Do Any Chore To Be In Different Room Then 'Beloved Toddlers'

2. Remarkably, 41 Year Old Man Honestly Believed Bathrooms Only Needed Cleaning Annually

3. Kids Cry Inconsolably When Its Dads Turn To Put Them To Bed

4. Despite Assertion That Its Not A Problem, Local Dad Can't Unclench Teeth So He Drinks 8th Coffee of the Day Through Straw

5. Dad Repeatedly Responds 'No' to 4 Year Old's Requests for Him to 'Play with me?'

6. Despite Near Constant Grumpiness Family Still Harbors Tender Feelings For Patriarch

7. He May Say He Is a Man, But Fathers Skill Set Does Not Support Such a Claim

8. Lacking Any Self Awareness, Dad Claims He Could Still Run with Guys In NBA

9. Impressively, Dad Maintains Vanity Despite Having Developed Classic 'Sitter's Body'

10. 'Man of a Thousand Jokes' Discovered to be Man of Merely 4 Jokes Told and Retold Thousands of Times. Two of them are Puns.

11. One Man's Journey To Truly Alarming Personal Hygiene Habits

12. Watching Television Constantly is One Family Tradition This Dad Intends to Pass On

Home, Home!

They all start the same.

Teddy is the alarm clock. He is two and a half years old. This age comes with many challenges for the little guy and can lead to many challenging moments for us. It's all okay though as evolution has whittled away at this problem for some time by now and as a result he is in possession of nature's cutest adaptation. He is unbearably adorable. All cheeks and just enough language to get his point across eventually after several missed guesses, while giving your heart if not your countenance a smile as you try to interpret his barely understandable babble/speak. Even if the way he pronounces a word like 'truck' is mortifying at first, it's also sweet beyond words. So his morning cries (more often then we tend to admit coming from the space between us in our bed) are tolerated.

The first instant is the only challenge. How can you possibly be waking up this early, you think. But he is anything if not persistent. His insistence makes you open your eyes. The fog lays low for a bit, we are almost 5 years into this schedule however and we long since have stopped cursing the morning light. Before you know it the blurred vision takes focus and he is there, all cheeks and sorrow that we are not yet awake and feeding his belly and his need for attention. Momma never asks for relief from this duty. She knows I'd help, at least most of the time, but she loves the morning light with her coffee and her soon to be giddy and happy boy.

It's her story to write, the story of the morning the two of them share, but I love what I walk into when I go downstairs anywhere from 20 minutes to an hour later. He is curled up under her arm, laughing and silly, every bit the showman. His belly and life are full at the moment as he's been afforded the chance to be Mommy's only for a few minutes each day. They both love it.

Before coming down the stairs I open the door to Charlie's room. I turn off the white noise and allow our low key morning fun to drift up to him, allowing him to wake gently. On the good days, on most days, we'll hear something like, 'Mommy. Come get Me.' at full on four year old volume 10 or fifteen minutes later. Mommy comes eventually, or if he has to wait a minute he might come down on his own. Either way the morning is in full swing by now, taking a turn from the rhythm of a 'home day' into the reality of a 'school day'. They don't know that yet. We do. It's also a work day and we need to dress and make lunches and dress the guys and prep for the day. So the TV goes on. The boys sit silently on the couch, cereal and sippy in their laps while George or Sponge Bob more recently, entertain us as well as them. We are fully engaged viewers of TV for children and we know when somethings good or not. It's mostly not, but these two we like.

Our slow and soothing rhythm steadily increases in velocity. What we would allow to occur organically earlier in the morning now has two parents prompting and prodding if not begging for them to move move move. It's a bummer for everyone involved. Mommy and I frantic to make deadlines, some real and unavoidable, some self-imposed, all interfering. By the time we sit in our cars we know that the bubble was burst, but we never can actually notice it while it's happening. The weekend is over and we all have to get on with what it is we get on with.

'Is today a home day, Daddy?' Charlie will ask. He and Teddy both wait for the answer.

'Nope. Sorry, buddy. But it is a school day! You get to see all your friends!' And it's true. He loves his school friends. We all do. But eventually has asks how long until another home day. We answer together, I start.

'School, school, school, school, school...' and I look to him in the rear view mirror.

His eyes get wide and he's so happy to speak up for his part. 'HOME, HOME'

Our New World

I remember with great fondness, even a touch of longing, the Saturdays we had before we had kids. They started late in the morning. From this vantage point, as parents of a toddler and a four year old who is a part time toddler, the time we started on weekends was decidedly not late morning. In fact now it would be decidedly midday.

We didn't need to plan like we do now. The coffee maker was not prepped the night before. In fact it was such a carefree and wondrous time that we might not even have carved out space in our brains to know whether or not we even had coffee to brew. What care we? We lived in a city, the city, New York, and there was always every version of coffee just outside the door. When your only burden is two large coffees to shake the cobwebs off of last night you really don't care about the four flights of stairs. Why would you.

We'd cook large breakfasts. Maybe we'd fill the large bowl, the deep one that didn't fit in with the set, with cherries. They show up early in spring. Always a surprise. We'd leave the bowl on the counter until the day made its lazy way to the living room and they'd come with us, half eaten with pits sinking step by step to the bottom of the bowl with each cherry taken. Sometimes they made it to the evening out on the coffee table. They'd be left there as we left for coffee and strolled, never knowing we wouldn't be back until late in the evening, after the last song Dirty Mac and the Bumper Crop Boys would play at the bar we'd never been to, that we strolled into to drink and conversate. It was no day to be strict with language, we would 'converse' at work, but over pints of Frambois/Guinness with our new favorite band we'd never hear from again, we definitely were conversatin'.

Saturdays took different turns to magical outcomes. They were all of a piece, these years when we could capture magic. Boring Saturdays that would border on the mundane often wandered and found something approaching bliss. Sometimes we found ourselves afloat in it. Other times we knew we both wanted something specific. We'd have our coffees, our breakfasts, perhaps an exercise and we knew we had to go get it. Head where we knew it lived. One of us would say, 'You know what I'd really like to do?' and without fail the other would guess correctly, 'Go to New World?'

We lived in the impossibly eclectic and diverse borough of Queens, in the vibrant Astoria neighborhood. Our food options were frankly limitless. But for us the place was always New World. A two and a half hour drive up into the Catskills to a pretty, rural, though easily accessible stretch of road between the picturesque towns of Woodstock and Saugerties. In our case 'easily accessible' was relative. I had a car for the summer months that was rented for me by my employer. Other times, and this is certainly crazy, we would find the cheapest local rental place and rent the car for the day. Yep. These are the decisions you can make before kids. Pretty fabulous, right.

We loved New World. The food was fabulous. Slow food, done right and creatively. It was a safe place for us to try new things as there was nothing they offered that wasn't delicious. It was high end food in a shorts and t-shirt establishment. Gourmet kitchen in an old mountain farmhouse. It's just great.

The other part of those days that lives now in my mind was the glorious absurdity and extravagant indulgence, the wide eyed romanticism of us taking the day to travel for a decadent meal and time together. We'd have every course offered, bread and white bean dip, blackened string beans with remoulade and *then* we'd get appetizers. Drinks and meals and desserts and coffees, even an espresso. All in cargos and your favorite T-shirt put on fresh so as not to be crass.

When we had a pain that felt truly life altering we drove there to wallow and tear up and hold hands and celebrate what we still had. When we wondered if we should change this wonderful life by having kids, those days of absurdity served a purpose. We'd debate, taking turns taking either side. It was on one of those rides that we agreed that the argument that took the day was that having, at least trying for a family was an opportunity to experience an essential and fundamental aspect of being human and with the little time we had left we owed it to ourselves to try. It was on these rides that we nervously considered being mom and dad while escaping New York for a piece of magic and Seitan Steak and a Mother's Milk. It was on these rides that we solidified what was our reality.

When it came time to plan a wedding I was unfortunately not up to the task. I was foolish as many men without the responsibility of family by their mid-30's can be. I resisted and made difficult for my bride some of the things that should have not even been issues, instead causing her additional challenges asking for compromise when I was truthfully insisting we do certain things my way. By far the thing I regret the most was nixing the photographer. Because despite all of the challenges I may have caused for us in the lead up, the day was amazing. The greatest day of our lives to that point. The easiest part of the planning was where to get married. New World.

We haven't been in years. Not since before the kids. Our new world, the one of diapers and cuddles and bedtimes and family life is magical and amazing and is one I shudder to think we considered not discovering. But from time to time I can't help remembering the magic we could make all on our own. The magic we could make for ourselves and for each other.

5 Lessons Learned While Hiding In The Other Room

Have you ever taken a step back and tried to understand your toddlers understanding of the world? If not take a minute sometime to just observe. You might be surprised by what you find.

From time to time I am home alone with the boys for an hour or two on the weekends. It's not often, but it happens and when it does I do my best to hide from them observe them from afar to see what I can learn about what they know. Here are a few of my conclusions.

1. **You *don't at all* have to teach a child to hate** - To the contrary. They come to it quite organically. That said, they have nary a care to your race, creed, sexual orientation or income bracket. Their sole determining factor between love and hate is whether or not you are giving them what they want when they want it. Furthermore, as toddlers, this may still result in them hating you. Granted, they have only the most vague sense of 'hate' and likely mean something more like, 'I'm mad at you', but still they are perhaps the demographic least afraid

to hate. Granted, it's usually balanced with cuddles but still.

2. **They are intuitively aware that possession is 9/10ths of the law** - At least when they possess a thing. When someone else is in possession of something, and really it can be anything, that to falls under the category of things that are rightfully theirs because at one point they were holding it. Our four year old likes to say it was his 'from when I was a baby.'

3. **Sharing is not a virtue, it's a liability** - This is mostly in regard to toys. My son told me yesterday that he wanted to play a game in which the only rules he could articulate were that '..all the toys in the world are mine.' I'm not paraphrasing. He was so proud of himself for inventing this game. He thought he'd cracked a code or something.

4. **They have a sense of natural law** - You use what you got. In our case we have two boys, 4 and 2. The big one is huge and he uses his hugeness to appropriate property of the younger one, be it land or durable goods. The little one, he's crazy. It's like he's in prison and he knows he has to act insane from time to time to keep the bigger one a little off balance and afraid to come after him. It's an

intricate dance, but one that's mostly entertaining and remarkably effective.

5. **They are aware of how adorable they are** - Seriously, they know. They know that eventually we'll break, whether it's a laugh or a cuddle or all out crying, they on some level know that we are powerless over them in the end. Thankfully they tend to go about their days happy and grant us the illusion that we are in charge. I think they pity us.

There is a good deal more to learn, but for now, I'm just going to hide in watch from the other room and hope they don't hear me. Besides if they see me gorging on these Skittles I'll have to share.

30 Years Ago, 30 Years To Go

When I was eleven years old life was pretty damn great. I was finally able to play on the CYO team where I was the star everyone saw coming. I was finally allowed to leave the school where I was punched more than I'd have preferred and was instantly popular in my new school, where I wouldn't catch a punch for a good five years. Girls, girls I was starting to notice almost all noticed me! Of course one or two didn't, which was also great because that allowed me to talk about them for hours on end with my best friend Cory while we shot hoops, rode bikes, got into trouble and hung out every day. I remember it like it was yesterday. The map of the streets, and all the little curbs you could catch air off of, and all the paths through woods, the towpath along the canal that could take you uptown to the theater that played matinees of 'Back to the Future' that I'd bring myself to after earning money mowing the lawn. The locks that everyone else jumped off but I was too mature (scared) to and the trail into the woods where parents didn't venture and where we taught ourselves to smoke cigarettes. If there was nothing to do for some reason I had a basketball court across the street that was essentially mine for years where everyone came to play. Hoops on either end but we only ever used the one side, the one with the net that came off, then the chain that went in its place only to become half destroyed and half tangled so you couldn't get that satisfying sound of the chain swish when the ball made it through. It's all engraved in my brain. It was 30 years ago. And it feels like I'm still there.

30 years from now I'll be in my 70's. I fully intend to be vibrant and present and years away from my final farewell. But still, your 70's are your 70's. My great accomplishments will have been achieved, whatever they might be. And don't kid yourselves. Anyone that makes it to their 70's has had their fair share of great accomplishments. They've had a fair share of everything, actually. They've had love and loss. They've had wins and losses. They've had boundless optimism and crushing defeats. They've had magic. They've had insurmountable challenges that they prayed to be saved from only to find out how capable, how able, how great they actually could be. They've learned that most of the tragedies are actually just turning points. They've survived what they thought would kill them. Maybe physically, maybe spiritually maybe just situationally, which often feels the worst but leaves the least scarring. They've bought and sold and bought. They've seen cruelty. They've been moved to tears by beauty and by rage and by love and compassion. They've had a life.

It's impossible to think that I'm as far from 11 as I am from 71, but no matter how I crunch the numbers it always works out that way. Sadness is a small ingredient in this soup. Gratitude is the broth, the part that all the rest swims in. If I had to isolate a feeling I wish for you guys when you reach an age, it's gratitude. It's truly the key to unlock true acceptance, love and happiness. Because this gift you are given is not to be trifled with. I've seen people who didn't get it, who stewed in hate, anger, resentment and ugliness and it's not worth it. It's scary to be truly vulnerable but it's also necessary if you are going to ever be able to feel what all of this can be.

I started writing when I was not much older than 11. Back then it was the muse that would get to me. It might be months on end of filling notebooks or it might be years of living and reading and thinking and learning, not once putting pen to paper. Putting the pen to the paper was great. Not in quality of the work, but in the quality of the time spent producing that work. When there's so much to say, things you've only just figured how to articulate, so many things that you don't know how to keep all the plates spinning and fear you won't be able to get out this new piece of knowledge, this new way of understanding how the world is all connected, but it organizes itself, you let go of trying to hold on and you find yourself simply flowing. It's remarkable. It's playing pool on beers three and four, the angles appear to you effortlessly and you execute their plan intuitively and confidently. It's a jump shot going down for days, the hoop starts to look bigger, like it's looking at you and you know you can't miss. It's finding a task that excites you and becoming so enmeshed in it that you lose awareness of yourself and function fully engaged. It's a way of refreshing yourself to be so fully immersed. It feeds you and gets you back to full. It's a glorious feeling that has occurred to me at the keyboard and with my open notebook. I hope you both find something that replicates that feeling. It's so gratifying.

I shared it with a handful of people from time to time. It was hardly their fault that they didn't fully understand the task they'd been assigned. They were to merely report that it was brilliant. Transcendent. Perhaps they could have questioned what it was I was doing wasting time working when I was sitting on a goldmine with this massive and massively beautiful talent. Instead they said hurtful and mean things like, 'It's really very good. I really like it.' I eventually would recover and write about how cold the world can be to an artist.

Then you two came along. Turns out you guys were just the kick in the ass I needed to start living the life I talked about wanting. I started with a terrible first attempt at blogging while mom was pregnant with Charlie. Writing has always been my way of logging memories. Not just of events, but also of experiences. Of feelings and thoughts.

And even in the excitement before I met you, at the mere thought of meeting you someday, I had to start building my collection of memories up. But I couldn't do it. I'm embarrassed actually by the things that were there. I'm not kidding when I say this, I was literally the only person to have ever seen this blog. Even your mom, who was kind and supportive only heard what I read to her.

That fear of being fully exposed, the fear of being vulnerable in front of people, it owned me. Not just in what I had written but in life. My life was in service to never feeling vulnerable and exposed. Ultimately it's a goal you can accomplish and many men do, but it's a goal you'll regret achieving. Its fool's gold. As men you need to know, feelings are often hard for us to understand and to recognize, but when you do notice something don't succumb to the foolishness of thinking you can outrun yourself. You can't. That game is rigged. You can't avoid feeling vulnerable or exposed. If you do you might make it through protected, but you will have lost the only opportunity you have to live a great life.

Sure, I am a proud father and I would not at all be surprised if you accomplish a great many things in life that would make your resume a thing to be envied. But I can tell you right now at 2 and 4 you each have the chance to have a great life. A beautiful life. But if you hide from life, avoid pain and discomfort, try to keep who and what you are covered up, you'll get to the end and realize you wasted the whole damned thing. I'm so thankful to you both for being the unwitting teachers who clued me in to this.

Before that it was your mom who crumbled the walls. She helped me understand that I had to stop hiding from life. Which I did actively until she helped me engage and be vulnerable in front of just one person. Her. In doing so I saw what I'd been missing.

Writing here has taken many turns I didn't see coming when I started. I've had some successes and it's been great. I hope there are more. But in the end, this, the developing dad blog is about you guys. Even the parts that are so clearly about me and my journey. Someday I'm not going to be here and you're going to be left with an understanding that you didn't know as much about me as you wished you did and it's my hope that this can be a small supplement to your record of me, mom and our family. Not just when I'm passed, but before that as well.

I want you guys to have the chance to read about how we were with you each and how much we loved you. How obsessed we were with you. I want you to know who I was growing up. I want you to know that I've made huge mistakes and lived to tell about it. I want you to know that I've been really depressed for long periods of time and even thought about ending it all. I've even taken comfort knowing it was an option. Then I want you to read about the amazing wonderful life I got to live instead. I want you to know that therapy is something you can do. It's like working out and eating right. Therapy can be part of being healthy and you should never ever feel anything is beyond repair. I want you to know fully, from my own words how flawed and human I was. I want you to know that I was funny. Sometimes in really inappropriate ways, though I'll probably hide most of the really blue material (*I also want you to know I love old phrases that were not even a part of my life, but once found I incorporated them into my language, things like 'blue material.'*) from you guys. I want you to know that I made bad decisions and that none of them were as bad in the end as they may have seemed at the time. I want you to know that I had a big heart and my work meant something to me.

I want you to have a chance to meet the me of 41 and hear about what I thought about. I want you to have a place to go if you're ever curious about whom I was when I was growing up. Your parent's voices are your native language and I want you to have this always here so you can hear my voice in your head saying my words to you when I'm gone. I want you to hear me say I love you, Charlie, with all my heart. I want you to hear me say I love you, Teddy, with all my heart. I want you both to know how much this life has meant to me because I got to be your dad. I want you to know I just cried a little after saying that.

I want you to have all of this, all of me for as long as you want it. I want to be there in the only way I can be at the times you'll wish I was there but know I can't be.

I love you with all of my heart, Teddy.

I love you with all of my heart, Charlie.

Hell Found Me at the County Fair

Saturday we found ourselves, all of us, lost amidst the deep weeds of toddlerhood.

We were leaving the county fair. It was hot, crowded, noisy and uncomfortable. This was the setting as I did my own performance piece re-enacting every episode of cops ever. The big one was melting while the little one was overdone and riding his big brother's coat tails. All the mistakes that can be made were. We were unprepared for the crowds, the food, the animals and the heat. Naps were skipped and bad behavior was mollified with treats. In hindsight any parent of any ability could have predicted the outcome. We could have predicted it. But we chose instead to barrel through because that is what you do with toddlers. If you waited for optimal conditions you'd be frozen in place, TV blaring, hiding from your kids. Forever.

Instead we took them to the fair where hell found us. It's not the fault of the fair. It's not the fault of the heat and it's not the fault of the various vendors and tricksters hanging their sweet booty, in the form of plush Spiderman dolls or blow up SpongeBob's to attract the hearts and minds of the world's most brutal and successful class of negotiators, toddlers. Actually it's totally the vendors fault. And of course the toddler's fault. Everything is their fault. It isn't their responsibility to do anything other then what they do, but let's not kid ourselves, we're all grownups here and it's ALWAYS the toddlers fault. That's okay, they can hardly be blamed for it.

Back to our story...

As I sit on the vacuum packed, stifling, Twinkie-shaped, sardine can of a school bus with all manner of humanity, waiting on the edge of my seat to see if one of us will crack, scream and dive out the window as the bus tries to weave its way through the throngs of fair goers oblivious to those of us on the bus and our plight, toward the traffic that it will have to navigate before getting us to our abandoned vehicles in a vast empty field 3 miles away, I felt relief that at least we were nearly done with this trial. I believe that life tests you and it looked like we were going to make it out of this one having passed this test and learned a lesson.

The bus eventually picked up speed as we traveled away from the fairgrounds. A breeze moved the still hot air and we all let our shoulders down a bit. Even the enjoyable parts of such a day, for parents, are challenging. An example? The Butterfly's. Going into the netted area, filled with flowers and butterfly's was something like magic. Until you try to control a 4 year old and a 2 year old that don't really get it. We were given small, foam style paint brushes upon entering and were told they were dipped in nectar to attract the butterflies, which the 4 year old could eventually do. I turned for a second to look and marvel at how he had managed to procure a butterfly for his very own enjoyment. Being four and having the attention span of a gnat and needing the validation of constant achievement at video-game speed he was bored nearly immediately, which was fine, I still had to look after the 2 year old. Where the hell did he go! Ah. There he.. wait. Teddy, no! He had started brandishing his brush like a weapon and was trying to in fact 'squish' the butterflies. Thankfully he is not as coordinated as he thinks he is and no butterflies were harmed in the making of this disaster. In the future, even later that day, this was the memory we isolated and highlighted as the 'magic' part of our trip to the fair.

As I slowly drove the air conditioned car I had a few moments of serenity on my way back to the fairground to pick up my wife and kids. A thought snuck into my mind. I could probably get away with sneaking off for a bit. Have a beer, catch an inning or two of the Mets game. Why not. What would they care if they got to stay at the fair for a few more minutes? Kids love fairs!

Having arranged with Karen to have the boys across the street from the gate through which we entered the fair I knew it was not to be. They were waiting and I had what they needed. A car, some screens (I don't care what you think about this, keep it to yourself, talk behind my back, just don't think I care about your data and research) and a ride back to the grandparents' house.

I'm afraid that my abilities as a writer will fail me as I try to describe what it was I returned to. The fairgrounds are in a rural area and the lawns of the residents of the modest homes in surrounding the grounds are filled to bursting with cars that paid a bit extra for the convenience. These folks who paid $10 to be able to leave immediately, when free parking was right down the street, people I called suckers not 3 hours ago, are the smartest people ever. As we crowded our car onto the edge of one such lawn, across from the parked police car, lights aglow for apparently no reason other than to be prepared, my family came into sight. The full blast of a Volvo AC unit with the windows up can completely cancel out the sounds of what was perhaps the busiest moment of the busiest day of the county fair, megaphones ablaze, kids screaming from death defying rides and all manner of annoying, ice cream truck style circus music blasting from the concourse that is perhaps as much as 25 feet to my left. What it can't obscure is the wailing and screaming of my four year old son, retreating to the maze of automobiles behind him, blood curdling screams that would cause me, you and any other decent person to stop and watch to be sure that he is not in mortal danger.

He is not, but it's not so evident. You see, I'm angry now. Again, it's unfair, not his responsibility and still entirely his fault that I'm now on a warpath. He's a big four year old and his brother is squirmy. Being outnumbered and overburdened by the necessary and unnecessary items that accompany a mom of toddlers from a fair, my wife was not able to fully gather him in his state and it was a full blown disaster unfolding. I kid you not, everyone stopped, as if this were a real episode of cops, and watched as I stormed, cheeks ablaze in frustration and fed-uppedness as I marched directly at the boy and restrained him physically. This was a situation in which diplomatic methods could not be employed, not yet at least. We were in the midst of a full blown rebellion. What was needed was a police state, removal by force and I was the brute squad.

Here I was, a stranger in a strange land, looking to all the world like the type of father I was, but not the type I reported to be. I prefer to be the benevolent dictator, allowing my boys to think they have choices. 'Do you want to brush first or read a story first?' that kind of thing. But when the moment is upon us, when hell is staring me down at the county fair all artifice is lost. This is a regime that must occasionally use the full force of its bestowed powers and put down all threats. Today that threat came from within and I'm terrified to think what the surrounding masses thought of our little performance. Surely they saw my anger, his frustration, our failures and must have come to the same conclusions I've often come to when seeing others in this or other, similar situations.

Within five minutes, a seemingly short time until you've spent it confined in a station wagon with two screaming, not shouting, SCREAMING toddlers, we were able to diffuse the situation using the wisdom of our elders who always have spoils ready for their grandkids visits.

'Okay, Charlie. I guess I should call Grandma and tell her to put away the cupcakes and ice cream. Cancel the pancake dinner. Charlie doesn't want it.' I said in my best toddler-whistle falsetto.

Deep breaths. Wiped tears.

'No. I want cupcakes.'

'You do?' I asked.

'Yeah'

'Okay, I'll tell Grandma, as long as you're a good boy and say you're sorry to mommy.' Still falsetto.

'I'm sorry, mommy. Yeah!' he shouted, and got the attention of the other.

'Cupcakes!' They yelled in unison.

A Circle Never Ending

My writing is strongly influenced by both of my parents. If I were to try to view my writing through my parents eyes, and if I were to remove the silly and the angry and the opinionated pieces and evaluate the heartfelt, meaningful writing I've done I believe each of my parents would see heavy influences from the other. This reflects an instinct to generosity and humility combined with a true admiration and fascination with each other that defines them as far as I can see. My father would point to the emotional presence and depth of humanity in them and throw credit to my mother and my mother would point to the thoughtfulness and the ability to design the contours of my tales to emphasize a perspective, to land on that perspective in a more impactful way and credit my father. I would say it's the only way I can be having been born of these two. Having been so makes me appreciate greatly that which is beyond ones control. The luck, the accident of birth and who it is we are made of.

Developing Dad was consciously conceived of as a place to record this whole experience. A place set aside to dwell on what it is and who we are as we become the family we will have been. I hoped in inception that it would be a place we can come to as we get further and further away from this time of transformation and visit the selves we were. It is designed as thoughtful nostalgia and on that front I think I'm reaching my aim. Maybe not exactly as I conceived of it originally, but honestly and presently. What I didn't think of initially was the unexpected audience I would have who would mean so much to me.

I have many moods and states of being and over time they are all on display here. Sometimes I feel like being funny. Turns out wanting to be funny is much more in line with angry than I'd ever imagined, but the more I write the more I learn about me. Other times I want to be clever or even intellectual. I'm a bit defensive about being smart. I don't feel like I am, but I see it in the pieces I go back to. I'm not entirely sure of my intelligence. You can tell by how incredibly confident of it that I am. I mean, I never question my intelligence. There's a reason for that.

Then there are the times I'm naked. When I shed my many cloaks and reveal the thoughts and feelings I have that are genuine. The part of me that's with me in each second. The ugly and the beautiful and the scared and the strong and the weak. Me. It turns out that I'm most excited to share this with my parents. It took having kids to understand what my parents were. I suppose I've had an ongoing relationship with 'who' they were, one that persists to this day and I suspect will live in me long after I've said my goodbye's to them. The relationship I have with my parent's lives within me. It's too much to think of the days ahead when I won't be able to hug and hold them, but these days are inevitable. But my ongoing relationship with my mom and dad is so ingrained within me that it will never disappear as long as I'm here. It will be small solace I'm sure, but true nonetheless. The great joy I feel that they have read my most intimate thoughts and seen vulnerabilities that they might never have been able to hold and reassure is amongst the greatest gifts I've ever received. I'm so heartened to know they've taken the time to know me in ways that frighten me to be known. To know that they are ever more loving and tender despite different outlooks or views on life. To know in my bones that they love me, the real me, the me I get to be here and can't always present to the world, is a gift I will never take for granted.

We are all adrift in a sea of life, each of us can look to either direction and see the immutable and inevitable parameters of our existence. From the middle of what is a standard scale life, one not guaranteed for another second, but expected to last about as long as it already has, I find times when new life is the prevailing current. Other times the far shore leading to lands unknown, unexplored where we, if we are lucky, drift off to at the end of a long and adventurous journey is the overwhelming reality. Overwhelming because goodbyes and endings are far more painful then beginnings and hellos. More overwhelming because they compel us to make meaning. At first the task is to make meaning from the end itself. But ultimately we discover that despite the endings enormity and sadness, the meaning doesn't live there. We all come to understand that while it is now in the past, the meaning of the tales we finish, the ones we see through the finish line are within us. Of us. In a sense this is the meaning of eternal life. All of it, bestowed upon me is the cumulative love and life of all those that have come before me. And now I get to garnish this feast of meaningfulness and hand it down to others who will pass it on. Whether to their own offspring or to the love of life that inspires those that simply see them, love them, admire them and are loved by them. It's a circle never ending.

5 Ways Being a New Dad is Just LikeBeing a Rock God!

I used to think being a dad was trading your high tops for comfortable sneaker-shoes, exchanging drinking 'til 3 and sleeping til noon for reruns of *The Big Bang Theory* and sweats, and retiring your cock, leaving one with a sad and flaccid penis—once your resplendent staff, now a very utilitarian pee stick.

Now that I am a dad I see that it's much more like a Charlie Sheen meltdown or the life I imagine to be lead by whoever the fuck, you know, the guitarist from the stones...inspiration for Jack Sparrow. The guy.

I typed this and all of the above while going commando and approaching 36 hours in the same t-shirt while wearing slippers. In public. How do I pull off such brazen disregard for common decency?

Easy. I'm a dad.

(Keith Richards. That shit was bugging me. Which brings me quite organically to the first way being a dad is the same as being a rock god in the 70's.)

I have somewhere around a hundred lonely, starving, barely surviving brain cells left

Ever seen *Festival Express*? It's a great doc made with amateur footage of a festival doomed from the start by romantic designs made in a room with thick, rust colored, shag carpeting with smoke and lava lamps filling the air. The Grateful Dead, The Band, and Janis Joplin hanging out on a train touring across Canada. I think Sha Na Na may have been there too. Why not, this was destined to be a carnival. The scenes at night are incoherent and filled with soulful but bad music and tons of laughter. It's awesome. Everyone is clearly stoned to the bejesus belt. I feel like now, having had just two boys in the last four years, that I would totally fit in with this crowd of burnouts and eccentrics.

These are now my people.

Personal grooming

I'm talking seriously personal. I used to worry about how that shit looked. I used to keep it high and tight. I may have even dabbled in scents at some point. Must have been the 90s as I'm pretty sure it was Drakkar. In any case, I'm now looking like a 70s pornstar. A European pornstar, even. Seriously, my privates now have what I like to call the "Reggie Watts." He's a great comedian and musical genius, or vice versa. Whatever. Google that shit. You'll see what I mean.

I have groupies

Not at all like Penny Lane with Stillwater, but still. The boys have the ability to manipulate me emotionally at every turn and always do so while reinforcing my male ego by literally thinking I can make the sun come or go. They have confused me with Zeus and I'd gladly stand on a roof, declare myself a "golden god" and jump into the pool before them.

I have no shame

None. I had no idea you could feel this free. I once went a full three weeks without showering.

By the end of the night I'm covered in bodily fluids often of unknown origin

Puke, blood, numbers one and/or two, boogers: the two year old has become quite a frat boy lately and gets a real kick out of the reaction I have when he spits on my face. I mean, they're the cute spits, the kind that make a funny sound and are really more like zerbert's, but it's still spit. He likes to get it in my eye.

Us dads may not have gotten there in the same way, but really, how much does it matter. I'm a great god and I have and shall retain dominion over my subjects for upwards of a decade. Until then I'm living like Keith Richards. And when people see me they'll all make jokes about how amazing it is I'm still alive considering the hardcore lifestyle I'm clearly living based on my disheveled, haggard and clearly coming undone look. This will fill me with a perverse pride of sorts. Until I get in the Volvo, covered in dried, pureed organic fruits with "The Wheels on the Bus" blasting from the speakers.

Screw it. I'm getting these kids to bed so I can watch a TBS marathon of *Big Bang*.

Handle with Care

I sometimes take a picture of you because you're just so adorable and amazing and beautiful. And sometimes I catch a hint of fragility in what the camera catches. Other times I see huge heaping mounds of it. Giant reserves of delicate. Like you're a crystal chandelier in the shape of my beautiful boy. And then, in my mind's eye, I see all the thousand ways you'll be disappointed by the realities of life you can't even fathom at this point. Sculpted from this thing of beauty into another thing of beauty to be sure. But still, that journey is treacherous and full of potential. Potential harm. Potential fortune. Potential damage and grace.

Maybe it's you. Maybe I'm not just a proud dad that's just insanely obsessed with my kids. Maybe *your* specialness, *your* perfectness is not a function of my pride. Perhaps you are magical and I'm afraid of being at the helm and breaking you by some silly decision I make that seems necessary that I'll grow to regret years from now.

I could stare at the pictures of you, the you you are now, on the precipice of independence and I dread the pain that growing up can be.

You'll be fine. I know that. But you'll be broken too. You have to be. Good, happy little boys can't survive growing up. If they could they'd never grow up. This sounds good until you realize that never growing up makes it hard to be a good man. That's just the way it is. It's okay. If you figure out what's important from being a boy you can pull some of those parts out and take them with you. You may have to pack them away for a time, but they will be there when the time comes and you need them again.

A broken arm is one thing. I can handle that. Easy, actually. But the thought of you being teased or picked on or not knowing what to do in a school cafeteria and feeling sick and disoriented because you think everyone doesn't like you, that thought ties me in knots. I got caught up in that process when I was a kid. I cried every day for months when I was sent to school the first time. I was removed eventually and allowed to return the following year, but by then I knew to be cautious. I knew people didn't like me. I knew they didn't have to. What was wrong, though, was that I looked at the few that enjoyed making fun of me and thought 'how can I do what they want me to do? How can I make them like me and stop picking on me?' All along there was a world of kids who'd have been delighted to play and be my friends. But I just kept trying to impress the cool kids, even shunning kids I'd have gotten along with great who weren't at the 'right' table.

Eventually I figured it out and sat safely where I didn't want to be. It was mostly fine and it largely defined who I was to the world, or at least to my classmates who comprised the entirety of the world for me then. It took so long for me to be the me I liked and was comfortable being. I learned early on how to make them like me and I leaned on that all the way through school, which I hated because of how it all began. I spent so many years not liking me, internalizing the voices of all the wrong people.

All because I had some tough early days. The types of days grownups like to say are 'tough but you get through them'. Days we fool ourselves into thinking aren't all that important because we were 5 and how much damage can really happen to a healthy and loved 5 year old. But we're wrong. We can get hurt and scar up in tender places at very young ages. Even those of us that had enough of everything. I see your precious face and your beautiful and awesome expectation that nothing breaks and everyone will love you always and it scares the hell out of me. Because some day you'll feel weird, alone and scared. And you won't know why. And it will break you as it must. In the end I'm afraid there's nothing I can do about the 'weird' and the 'scared'. You need to get through these things. We all do. But if we can help you with the alone part for as long as possible and stay present for the times you'll need to explore being 'away' than maybe, just maybe, a small but invaluable piece of you, a piece of the you you are now might be able to make it through to the other side. If it does I hope that you are able to see all the things that I'm getting to see in you. If you do you'll see what all that breaking was for. You'll know once again what it feels like to be a fragile chandelier. To look at something you love so much that you can't even imagine it ever not loving you back. The mere thought makes me break just a little.

Little Man, Big World

I complain, mostly for comic effect, but occasionally sincerely, about the extremities of emotions displayed by my boys, who are 4 and 2. It can be overwhelming and exhausting at times trying to keep up. But lately the older one's been starting to show shading. Middling not just between feelings but mixing them with thoughts and presumptions. Calculation and calibration. He's developing nuance and forethought. His communication can be veiled by strategy. He's different. He's becoming a bit more independent in thought, developing an inner life. He's becoming a little boy and revealing the nascent aspects of his character. The character he will be judged by independent of us.

All in all I'm sure it's not a very big deal. We are all separate people. It's a transition we feel lucky to be able to watch. We will be afforded endless opportunities to warn against danger, to praise the many wonderful examples we will surely see of his kind heart. We will be there to fight him when he *thinks* he's right and we *know* he's wrong. Hell, there's even a far horizon, one perhaps not as far as I imagine, when we will be there to fight him when he *knows* he's right and we *think* he's wrong. That will be another transition. For all of us.

But for a second I'm going to take a breath and be thankful. Stop to acknowledge how lucky we were before moving on to how lucky we are in a new, future present. Be thankful for the time when we were his everything. It's going to dawn on him soon that we're not infallible, but rather flawed. It's been nice for us to be his sun and him to be ours, all circling one another. Providing each other with all the power and light needed for an entire universe that exists in the spaces between us. Before he grew and his light couldn't be contained in our galaxy any longer.

There's still time. He's a very very big boy and often people think him much older than he is. Hell, sometimes we hold him to account like a kid twice his age. But he isn't twice his age. He's still a few months away from five years old. He may be the size of an eight year old but he's still naturally inclined to climb up onto my lap and tell me he loves me. He knows what it does to me now. Knows how happy it makes me. There's certainly something lost in the exchange now that he's aware of how his words affect me, but there's a ton more gained. His spontaneous proclamations of love were wonderful and pure. But the thought that he sees me and knows how happy I am made by him saying, 'I love you, Daddy' and he does so not only because it is true but also because he wants to exercise this newly discovered power of his to make me happy, that packs a pretty powerful punch as well.

We're going to do our duty bound best to foster his independence and we're going to try to teach him what we find to be most important; that he think about others and how to be a kind and thoughtful person. But for as long as we can, in the bubble that was once a universe, we're going to try our hardest to pay attention to the times when he isn't ready to be a small boy in a big world. When he wants to pretend like he's still a big man in a small universe. After all for all his eagerness to venture out he still needs to know that whenever he wants to come home and pretend to be the big kid in a two kid world he's always welcome. Besides, he'll quickly learn that doing that will make his Mommy and Daddy very, very happy.

I Wish I'd Met You Earlier

'If I could change anything I'd go back in time and meet you earlier so I would have more time with you.'

Of course for that to work I'd actually have to go further back than you might think. I'd have to go back to the relationships before I met you, to the therapies and jobs and life lessons and various family functions when I festered with free floating rage and self-loathing. The feelings that led me to some of the terrible decisions I made that left me looking for you in my early 30's via the internet, wasting one Saturday night after another with the wrong people engaged in the same search. And of course you'd have to go back and relive all you'd lived to get back to the same place at the same time. In the end even that wouldn't give us so much as a fighter's chance of creating the events necessary to ensure another 5-10 years with each other.

The truth is had we met earlier I wouldn't have been 'the one' yet and you may not have been either, though I have a harder time thinking that. Truth is we had to get to where we met, separately. In hindsight it was the only way it could have happened. Had you met me earlier you'd have met an even more imperfect man.

But we didn't meet earlier. Life knew when and where you were going to be and made sure that I was ready. Made sure I had resolved my old and musty issues and was better able to understand how little I knew. Made sure I had learned, even if only in theory, that the person you love and commit to is not meant to be the end of the challenges and the resolution of all discomforts but rather they are your help and comfort while facing them. Life made sure I knew that it was my job to be that for you, too. That the dream of finding someone to love and be loved by was not the equivalent of going on permanent vacation. That it was not your pillows fluffed and your sheets turned down and rooms cleaned magically and freshly stocked paper products everywhere you looked. It was not nonstop nights of endless passion and wine and late night bathroom window cigarettes and days full of endless entertainment.

Life brought us to the same place at a time when we were ready to commit. To face the challenges and monotony and joys and unknown glories of having someone to do it all with. To commit not only to someone that could make the highs pure bliss, but also someone who could endure the lows, tell you you're crazy and put up with the issues you haven't resolved. Someone who will love you if you never resolve them. Someone who can write all these things at 12:51 in the morning after we didn't have our best goodnight ever and never ever have to worry that

that means anything other than we each have to figure out what it is we have to apologize for. Because this is real. I'm forever thankful for you. You absorb my frustrations and reflect my joys. You make the bad times quick and the good times permanent. I hope I can do at least some of the same for you.

None of this could have happened any earlier than it did no matter how much later it was than either of us might have expected it.

That said it does leave me sad in one specific way.

I'm thrilled that Charlie is who he is and that Teddy is who he is. Specifically. Had it been another time they would have been other people. They wouldn't exist as we know them. So in that sense I'm so happy it happened when it did. But now I'm left looking at them and thinking...

'I wish I could have met you sooner so I could have had more time with you.'

It's impossible for me not to project out now that they are with us. It's hard to look down the road and know that at 20 I'm whispering to 60. The math gets more unnerving from there. I'm not going to live forever. It's something that hit me the second our first was born. Perhaps I'm dumb. We all know it doesn't last forever. To say that it occurred to me at the moment Charlie was born is to somehow suggest I hadn't known it all along. I did. I mean

I knew people died and I knew I was a person. So, ipso facto and ergo and whatnot. But not like now. Now I'm going to die on my kids. I mean, even in the best case scenarios I die and leave them behind. But at my age the chance is it's going to be when I would have been too young for my parents to go.

I didn't learn to even start appreciating my parents until my 30's. Not in the way they deserved. Not in the way that's a bit more reflective of the amazing job they did. And my god, I've needed them more these days than I can ever remember needing them. I understand how silly and sweet that sentiment must sound to them. I 'get them' now that I'm a parent. It must be cute to them to think I think I 'need them' now more than ever. Because those early days, my prehistory, the prehistory that is the equivalent to the one my kids are living now, concurrent with the peak of vibrant life for me are days they won't remember. They're our days, actually, not theirs. Theirs come later. And I was their third. Of six. And there were a few more. I have two and I've needed them for all of it.

It worries me to no end that I'll die while they still need me. The early days are just like that, and I'm still in the early days. But the deeper fear is that I'll die without them being ready, without them being of an age or established in the life that will be there's to live, that's the one I can't shake. I know no one is ever ready. I know I won't be. But

I'll have a home, a wife and a job and my boys. I fear leaving them before they have any of this. Before they have roots.

There's also a selfish piece to it all. I want to live long enough for them to forgive all the things we'll get wrong and to see us as people, who loved them all the way through, even through the hard times when they couldn't see why we did what we did. Through the times when we get it wrong. When they couldn't see the love that was at the root of it all. Because having kids and being a parent and a spouse, it's made me understand my parents in a way nothing else could. It made me love them in a way that's oddly equivalent to how much I loved them when I was just Charlie and Teddy's ages now, when they were my whole world and I was theirs and it made all of us special. There's symmetry now and I can see all that they did. I once again think of my parents as something so much more than 'just people'. It's your job to realize that they are in fact just people as you depart your family of origin. You have to see them for all their humanity and in that you find shortcomings and magnify them. It's a part of your liftoff you have to exercise. It's the balance to those years when they were the sun and the moon. It provides you perspective. But if you're lucky enough, like I am, you get to come around on that later and see how superhuman their lives have been. I'm back to a place where I can tell them unabashedly how much their love means to me. How much I love them. I want that with my boys. I want to make it there.

'I wish I'd met them earlier so we would have had more time together.'

The Misplaced Confidence of the Formerly Beautiful

Have you ever had a secret that was just too painful to share? I just know there's someone out there who could understand me if I could just get over myself. Just stop stopping every time I start to address it directly. Fear is cruel that way. It gets in and feigns ultimate power and you believe it. But it's all a charade. Any power fear has is usurped and misappropriated from its host. That power you feel being exerted on you, to apply the old horror movie trope, is coming from inside the house. Your house. You. The power is all yours and you have to claim it. As soon as you do fear will flee like the coward it is.

Here is my proclamation.

I am afflicted with the misplaced confidence of the formerly beautiful.

It may not be recognized in the DSM and there is likely not a ton of literature about this dreadful disorder, but for those few of us suffering from it none of that makes it any less real. It doesn't make it any less painful.

It's a pitiable reality I live day to day. One I don't wish on my most attractive enemies. Every night I'm tortured by my reflection, reminding me that those looks I've gotten, those looks I've come to rely on for my sense of self, from attractive young women, those looks are no longer intended the way I still, sadly, receive them in the moment. All day I've stolen glances of others checking me out. Now, when I see what greets there eye in the world of funhouse mirrors I now live in I am left little room for doubt that one of two things has happened. One, they are looking on me as an oddity here in these places of the young and beautiful I somehow still think I'm rightly placed in. Or, two, horrifyingly, they are not in fact looking at me, but rather 'keeping an eye on me' the old, thick, greying gentlemen who clearly doesn't belong.

Well I have news for you. Many of you will be me someday. Laugh. Go ahead, young beauties, but mark my words, beauty fades. Even on us, the most beautiful. You can only outrun it for a decade or two. Your number will come up some day. And when it does I hope you remember the way you look at me and judge me. I'm you, my friends. I'm you.

I too was able to claim a total and truthful lack of 'game' when it came to meeting the people I was attracted to. I was afforded all the free space on the high road. My best move was letting slip to a friend that I thought someone was cute. This actually led to nearly every relationship I initiated in my dating days. The other 90% were someone telling me that some other, similarly afflicted gorgeous person was interested in me. I never questioned. Of course they were. Then I'd decide if I was. If I was we'd date. For as long as I was into it. I assumed it was like this for everyone.

I was raised by humble and handsome people who didn't burden me with the knowledge of the appeal of my strong jaw line, piercing blue eyes, broad shoulders, alabaster skin and buttery smooth baritone. I was 6'2" and athletic on top of it. Lacking arrogance, I emerged in the world upon reaching majority a fully formed, devilishly handsome man free from the awareness of my native advantages over the average person. I assumed all people had yet to feel the bitter sting of rejection. Thinking it not at all unusual that someone might greet anyone with a sharp intake of breath followed by spitting out a phrase like, 'Wow. You're really good looking!' Didn't matter where I was, interviews and church and other formal settings. I just assumed this was a common courtesy between strangers raised with manners and good hearts. I assumed everyone would have to hold their bosses at arm's length. Out of respect for their dignity. I mean how silly would they have looked being rejected by subordinates. I always assumed my promotions were the same promotions anyone else would have received having dutifully arrived to work on time, answered most messages and was always available to smile and make small talk. These are the essential duties of handsome/good looking people after all.

But now, now I'm a fool. I still assume the never ending upward trajectory to continue despite having long ago settled into the middle. Thank god I met my gorgeous wife before my looks were so diminished. I managed to convince her, a fellow and currently gorgeous human, to marry me and quick. Before the fall of Rome as it were.

After a lifetime of the world and its inhabitants falling at my feet to help me over any and all challenges I didn't even realize that I am completely lacking the skills needed for someone in my current, hideous form. Thank god I managed to attend and graduate college while I still was on the path of least resistance, which is every path for the beautiful among us. At least I have a degree to fall back on.

But today, today is my day to take back my life, to swallow my humiliation and face the world. I'm thicker then I was and my profile in particular is to be avoided. My once prominent jawline is doughy. My broad shoulders have slumped and my skin is, well, problematic. But that is not going to stop me from being proud of myself. Today is the first day of the rest of my life. I'm going to eat better and care for myself more attentively. I'm going to run and use the elliptical and I'm going to do all the things everyone else has had to do forever just to keep up with me.

I may never be beautiful again. Lord knows I'll never be as stunning as I once was. But who knows. I'm to understand that men like myself can still get quite a bit from life if we can make it to 'distinguished', so there's still hope.

Dear Daycare, I'm Afraid You're Mistaken

I wrote this letter to my daycare before realizing that the 'teachers' at daycare have magical powers to transform my little monster into an angel. In my mind, the child they described to me was clearly someone else's.

....

Dear Miss Emily,

I'm so sorry to have taken so long to write this. It's just, well, embarrassing. For me and for you.

I'm afraid you've been giving me the daily reports of a different child in your care. I know. It's even embarrassing for me to tell you. But please know I'm not passing any judgment. I've been there. I have. I've actually corrected people on what a person's name was at my office only to find I was the one using the wrong name all along. I discovered my mistake when I chummily told Heather that the Kevin's had thought her name was Judy. Heather then blushed and told me her name was Judy. I was mortified for months. So I get it. Besides, I've known in my heart for weeks that this was the case, but it felt so good to get these wonderful reports that I let it go.

I don't know who is wrongly receiving Henry's daily reports, but at some point my guilt caught up with me. The poor kid, not to mention poor parents of the kid getting the mistaken reports detailing how their little love has inexplicably turned into a monster at your lovely daycare. The child you've been describing to us is truly an angel, and I shudder to think about how he's being fretted over at home at the news of the truly dreadful behavior that is being reported to his clearly wonderful parents.

We first became suspicious when, after a few days, the notes didn't change. "Wonderful boy! So well behaved and smart!" Later notes would describe a boy quick to share, easy to calm, and altogether a delight to be around at all times of day. Our Henry is bright, but the child you described, even in these fleeting notes, was clearly a boy we don't know.

You see, Henry, the real Henry, whom you clearly know by another name, is the furthest thing from 'well behaved.' In fact, if there's still any confusion as to whom Henry is, simply look around throughout the day.

Circle Time: He is likely screaming because A. you are reading the 'wrong' doggy book or B. you are reading the 'right' doggy book. There's really nothing to know other than the fact that he's screaming because you aren't doing what he wants you to or you are doing what he wants you to. It's a real catch-22.

Arts and Crafts: He is cracking himself up by pointing to his 'pee pee' and saying it's 'poopie.' We THINK he knows the difference and is being intentionally funny, but who's to say?

Playground: Judging by both my wife's and my personal experience, there's a 50/50 chance he's pushing or hitting someone right now. Or throwing rocks. I know the playground has rubber mulch under foot, but you'd be surprised at his capacity for finding throwing-rocks in the most unlikely places. Based on his appearance upon returning home, it's a safe bet he's the one that has gotten down to just his diaper and is rolling around in the rubber mulch. After that, it would seem he is trying to fit as much of the rubber mulch into his mouth as possible.

Lunch: If your menu ever varies from apple sauce and cheese sticks, he is yelling 'can't like it' while pushing his plate aside, sticking out his lower lip, and demanding apple sauce and a cheese stick. By the way, it's fine to give it to him. He tends to use the cheese stick for dipping. The boy you describe, eating and drinking everything offered, well, he sounds like a delight!

Nap Time: If we haven't outed our boy by now, this should do the trick. You'll know he's tired due to the amped-up grumpy combined with droopy eyes, yawning, and super clinginess. He WON'T be put down at this point until he's so asleep that you could actually toss him into the bed. This child you describe who naps from 1:00 to 3:30 daily is a literal dream come true. We seriously *dream* about this.

As a parent, I feel truly invested in all children, particularly those children roughly the same age as my own and living in the same area. These are the children who will make up my child's world, and from the sounds of things, you're doing an amazing job ensuring that the world my boy grows up in will be one filled with simply lovely children. Thank you.

Please accept my apology for allowing this to go on for so long.

All the best,

Henry's Daddy

The Couple Date, Toddler Edition

To be fair, you really should do this more often.

It's your semi-annual date night with people similarly afflicted with children in the 'rug rat' stage of development. You will only go out with couples in the same stage as you as there's just a hair more acceptance of your general dishevelment and lack of understanding of anything that has happened in the past 3 years that took place outside of your own home.

You start the night having properly timed everything, painstakingly, to be as together as you can be at the moment you are to arrive. And it's wonderful. You are Once again putting your best foot forward and demonstrating at least a modicum of pride in your appearance. It's such a foreign feeling that it gets you a little heady. Your hosts are in the same boat and the laughs and understanding of a person who gets what you're going through is intoxicating. You aren't crazy. Or you are, but it turns out you are supposed to be.

Before long you are on your second glass of wine and you are now well on your way to drinking like a college freshman again, ready to get sloppy and emotional and ready to call a taxi later to get you home. You're getting your drink on tonight. Having put more effort into this night than has been put into anything you've done for yourself in forever you determine that you just have to get going to that new 'high end' pizza joint downtown. There's no way you're getting this dressed up and not getting out, no matter how much fun you are having here.

Once there you see the line. Are you kidding me? You have a vague memory of a time when a line was a small challenge, a mere hiccup. A good one. One that spoke to something desirable at the end of it. This is purely a memory. There is not even a tiny residue of that feeling left, but none of you want to let the others down by being a drag on what's so clearly going to be an...

'To be honest, I don't even think there pizza's that good. I had it with some guys from work. It's not that much better than the place around the corner. No wait there.' you all dance around the idea for a minute before the 'thank god someone said something' moment happens and you all walk gloriously down the street.

You ask for the bar menu after being seated and noticing a disturbingly high number of families with kids there. It's alright. They ain't yours. You do miss them though and make a note that someday, when bathrooms aren't as urgent a need as they can be with little ones that seem not to understand the feeling of something coming, only recognizing its arrival, it might be a nice place to come for lunch with the kids.

No. Bar. You can bring your own though. The men head out and find a store and return wine in hand. Rather, wine in box in hand.

You're such a jackass.

Don't be silly. It's not the giant fridge box. We can put it on the floor. There's three bottles in here!

Turns out it's okay. You even see some presently-parenting-parents looking longingly. You offer, they demure. These are your people and lines are for suckers.

By the time you've sufficiently made it impossible to shove any more carbs in you realize you should be getting home. The kids are going to be up early and you need to get some Gatorade and aspirin down before getting to bed. These little ones make no distinction between weekday and weekend and six in the morning is extra early for a morning after.

So you all agree that you are tempting fate and should get home. You hug and shake and do the manly combo thing and tell each other you'll definitely do this again next week. Well, not next week, but certainly in the next month. If not then certainly sometime around the holidays. Or maybe just after, once all the travel is done. It's the kind of on the fly planning you do with friends when you are drunk. You are totally drunk, but you're a grown up now and that just means you have to hold it together.

Your cab comes and you give them your address and you laugh and flirt in the back and it's awesome. You're totally gonna have sex when you get home. But first you have to be dropped on the corner so you can chew some gum and eat some old Altoids so as not to smell like vagrants for the babysitter. You see them through the window, all adorable and in their jammies so you decide to hang out for a little. But they don't go down. Looks like they're waiting for you. You promise that once they are down you can meet up in the bedroom and 'finish' your date. You mean it this time. Seriously.

Your arrival is greeted with such excitement that you decide at least one half of a Curious George is probably a good idea. One or two. Before long you are bringing slightly calmed kids to their rooms and lying with them for a bit looking at the ceiling of green stars shone from the timed light on the dresser. You eventually notice that your eyes are closed and you haven't heard anything in minutes. You open and see the stars have timed out and he didn't even notice. His back is to you so you wait and listen. Breaths aren't deep enough yet to risk it. So you close your eyes and wait.

Finally you drift to sleep. It's okay. Same thing happened in the other room. It's not how you'd have scripted the date ending, but you'll take it. Every time.

We really should do this more often.

Becoming the One

There's a good many reasons I write. Most of them have evolved since I started Developing Dad. Initially it was motivated by my desire to make this thing for my kids. A record of who their parents were along the way. A place where they could go back and hopefully see how much they were loved. So they could learn from me while some of what I had to teach was still fresh in my mind. This is one of those posts.

My father is not always prone to giving advice. He's actively involved in helping us chew over a problem, but I think he takes a designers approach to most things having been a designer since far before he even had the degree to prove it. Or the career full of successes. He's a designer by nature before he was one by training. As such, and as a man that will often speak of how fascinated he is with his children and their perceptions and approaches, he revels in seeing us solve problems. Designers know that there are potentially innumerable ways in which to approach and resolve a problem and he loves seeing how others do it.

'I'm really very happy that you've chosen this life.' He said to me on the back porch of my brother's house the afternoon before our big day. 'It's a good life.'

It's a thought that's resonated with me. It got my attention in the moment and has held that attention now for going on 8 years. 'I'm really happy that you've chosen this life.'

It's not passive, I chose it. I chose to give love. I chose to accept it. I chose to look past fear and doubt and aimed at something beyond the immediate. I chose to commit to it. A thing I'm not sure I understood at the time, but a thing he knew far better than I, was something I'd grow into.

I'd come close before this a couple of times. In each of those earlier instances I walked away from the affair swimming in remorse over my shortcomings and failures. I wallowed in pity over the weight I didn't afford the relationships until it was too late. Until I'd messed up. In resolving these emotions, past years of recriminations and loud and repeated listening's to Rick Danko bleating out the lyrics to 'It Makes No Difference' or Dave Matthews singing sincerely about something I was trying to feel though I wasn't, I resolved and learned that I was going to have to accept that she wasn't the one. It was an important realization for me. To know that in the end while the pain was real when it was real and it was honestly desired when it was feigned the reality was that it was the fates and I had to learn everything I could from these painful experiences. In the end it wasn't meant to be.

Which is a total and utter cop out.

In the end of relationships you divvy up. The reality was, to a greater or lesser degree, or just in different ways for each situation, I was at fault. And the fault that was mine to own was that I wasn't the one. Not because I wasn't 'the one' per se, but because I didn't choose to become so. Not until the day after the day before my wedding when my father imparted wisdom he didn't even know he possessed.

He had made the choice, the commitment in his mid-twenties. He was on the accelerated plan of becoming a good man and becoming the one for the girl he'd marry. I drifted a bit longer. At least when it came to relationships and my ability to be who I thought I was.

'The one' barely existed on my wedding day. It also existed absolutely as much as it could. We were getting married after all. She was absolutely the one for me and I look back on that day often with the greatest of memories as it was the day when we set in motion the series of events that would bring about our unending happiness at becoming 'the one' for someone who was taking the same leap for us. The truth is that the love that brought us to that place, through a remarkable set of ups and downs was a precursor to a life we are now well on the way to completing the foundations of now that you are both here with us. But I was no more a pre-determined perfect fit for your mother than she was for me. What I was and am is madly in love with her. Which, yes, means I'm enamored of her. But more importantly it means I'm committed to her and she to me. Through the past seven-plus years of our marriage, through several challenging and seriously imperfect times where we have both failed each other and failed ourselves, we always rebound to that commitment and each time we do there is more trust, more love and more reason why we alone, specifically are the only partner that could ever be the one for the other. The ways multiply with each passing milestone of a life spent together figuring out what is meaningful to us and to each other. I'm infinitely more capable of being the one for your mother today as she is for me because of how imperfect life is and because we keep showing up for each other each day no matter how hard a day it might be. We'll continue to do so through fights and disagreements, through joys and celebrations, through the workaday drudgery that life can sometimes be, through laughs that become the special language we'll only be able to speak with each other that will give us endless capacity to carry one another when life strikes it's most painful blows. I could never have been the one for her in the way I am now when we were just starting out.

The concept of 'the one' is much maligned by the cynical and those lacking imagination. We all have times when we question its rightness and that's a part of figuring it out, but don't be fooled, 'the one' definitely exists. But like the rest of life it requires two things. First you have to be responsible for being the one and don't expect life to present to you 'the one.' That's not how it works. All you can control is you and if you want to find the one, go about being the one. That's the only way to know if you can in fact become the one for another. Second, go about being the one by showing up, every day, for that person you love. Apologize for your wrongs, celebrate the one you love and show up especially when it's hard to do so. If you don't you have absolutely no right to expect them to do so for you.

My father is a designer by nature and as such he has gone about accounting for a structure's integrity from inception. When he told me that he was happy that I chose this life, whether he knew it or not, that's what he was happiest for. He saw that I loved my bride fully and was happy that I chose this structure which hewed to the design he favored, built and tested in the life that he'd lead and was still leading, both beautiful in conception and structurally sound.

I was never so fool hardy as to think that there was one and only one meant for me. But I did seem to think that there were many ones and I just had to find one of them. I imagined that having that someone who loved me for me would make life easier somehow. And that I would do the same for her. I imagined that this would happen smoothly and easily as I simply had to find a person where this was true and I'd know they were one of 'the one's' for me. I wouldn't commit until then.

It was a fundamental misunderstanding of what love is, what 'the one' means. The one is not the solution. They don't arrive fit to your life. They don't come through the door and morph to some ridiculous, uninformed and frankly selfish version of what you think would be perfect. Instead they come through and you fall for them. That's it. The rest is up to you, up to you both, to make that moment mean something by committing and recommitting every day. Do that and you'll find you've found the one. The one and only one for you, fitting ever more perfectly together as you grow.

Unburdened

I've always been hypersensitive, which isn't something I've always been comfortable acknowledging.

When I was growing up it was a real issue for me. It's still a thing that can be hard for me. But as I get older, especially after having kids, it's practically unavoidable. When I was young everything I felt was turned into the only emotions testosterone could amplify. Rage, joy, jealousy, sadness or frustration.

Having feelings, being filled with emotion was terrible. The loss of control was awful. It felt vulnerable. It felt dangerous and I chose instead to express my feelings, at least the joy, jealousy and sadness ones through stoic denial of them. Which conveniently turned them all to rage and frustration. The two emotions I felt comfortable showing the world. Somehow those two feelings felt *invulnerable*.

But sadness was there at times. Sadness is still hard. It tends to come out as rage, but I can at least recognize it now. Jealousy is mostly gone. Sometimes I might feel a touch of envy but it's mostly for made up stuff like money. Sometimes I read something brilliant and wish I'd thought of it, but I don't know if that's jealousy.

The world instills in boys the misconception that painful feelings are the opposite of strength. They aren't. The fact that I couldn't kill them completely, those vulnerable, painful feelings are because they were important. They were protecting a part of me that couldn't be fully removed. No matter how hard I might have tried. The part of me that is ultimately my greatest strength.

The only feelings that can own me are those I hide. The ones I keep to myself. The ones that I'm afraid of people seeing.

I would never have believed that I'd ever have been comfortable sharing so much of my concerns and so many of my worries with the world. So many of my shortcomings, failings and feelings. I was invested in them staying hidden. I'd made them shameful by keeping them hidden. I'd made such simple and beautiful things as feelings and need and frailties and worries my undoing by being so afraid of them that I loaded them into my bones and my body and my bags and anything I could carry and then dragged them with me wherever I went. When they inevitably became too heavy and I'd become weary I'd crumble, drop it all in private, curse my weakness and then add that weakness to the pile that I'd once again pick up, pack on and carry around. It was untenable.

I don't imagine that I would have carried this burden forever. I imagine that some event would eventually have shown me the light and taught me that I needed to unburden myself. Perhaps it wouldn't have been an event. Perhaps it would have been the slow learning of a lifetime of pain that would have taught me my lessons and prodded me and encouraged me to finally let it go by putting it down, laying it out and sharing my load with anyone who'd care to see and take stock of it with me. I imagine I'd have gotten there some way or other had I not gotten there as I did. But thankfully I didn't have to wait for either of these things.

What let me know it was okay to be my entire person in front of the entire world was becoming a father. I have two sons who will grow up in a world that is prone to teaching its young men that 'manhood' means being more powerful than feelings of frailty and weakness. It's an unfortunate tradition and residual instinct of a time less enlightened than one I hope we get to someday soon. But until we do I need to be the proof that having feelings and being sensitive to them, all of them, rage and compassion and needing and passion and frustration and sadness and guilt and all of them, is a strength. It's in fact how you grow strong. Having feelings, expressing them, then putting them down is the only way to move on. It's my duty and my pleasure to show them this, to be the proof of this valuable nugget of earned wisdom.

More so than that even, it's my pleasure to show them gratitude for teaching me this lesson. For making my life so much more harmonious with the life that has been coursing through me that I could never fully come to grips with and feel comfortable in before meeting them and learning how to be brave and strong because of the love I have for them.

Thank you guys. You opened life to me. You made me strong enough to live it fully and honestly. You've made all of it, the joy and pain, pure bliss.

Things I Don't Give a Crap About Now That I'm A Dad

Since becoming a parent, so much has changed. I've found new depths of love. I've rethought and reordered my priorities. I've purchased a product called a 'snot-sipper' and been delighted at how well it works. I've found fears I never knew I'd have. I've learned that 'need' and 'want' are very different things.

I've also been imbued with a brand new 'superpower.' I now possess an endless supply of 'I don't give a shit.'

It's a delightful development, and it's an attitude that can be applied to so much in life. I really can't tell you how delighted I am to make this short list (the long list would be never-ending) of things that I, a dad to two toddler boys, truly couldn't care less about.

New Music: All my bands/artists are in their 50s at minimum and long dead in a good many circumstances. While I'm almost certain that the music industry continued past the mid-90s, I'm equally certain that I don't care and never will.

My Body: I think qualifying them as 'man-boobs' is so aspirational that it's misleading. They're just boobs at this point.

Kids: Other than my own, of course. They really seem great. I'm sure they are a lot of fun and just wonderful.

'The Real' Lives of Anyone: If your program's title begins with 'The Real...' you are lying.

Restaurants That Don't Have Kids' Menus: You're dead to me. All of you.

Your Thoughts on Gay Marriage: There is correct and incorrect when it comes to this one. If you are incorrect, there's no argument I can make that will change your mind. You'll have to do that on your own and in your own time.

Screen Time: Except for mine. Don't fuck with mine.

Helicopter vs. Free Range Parenting: I claim to bemoan helicopter parents. Meanwhile, I quit my job and changed career course midstream just to be able to take them with me to work. So, you know, not tons of consistency.

Consistency

Cleaning My Car: I prefer to just wish it were clean.

Debt: It weighs on me. It does. But really, am I going to stop buying groceries, paying the mortgage and not vacationing?

Teen Vampire Novels and Their Movie Adaptations: I have sons and will only try these things if they become interested. Not looking likely so far.

Movies Made in My Children's Lifetime: If it's a movie I can't access easily from my couch, watch mindlessly and drift in and out of sleep without feeling I missed too much, I have no use for it.

My Weight: This might be denial.

Your Opinion on My Parenting Style: Seriously. Get a life.

It's incredibly freeing to care so much about things that really matter now, like the two little humans I raise and their mom and to know that it's okay to officially stop caring about so much that makes no difference to their world.

You should give it a try.

A Love Letter To My Home

From the kitchen window in the house I grew up in you could see my lawn. It stretched out flat like a sheet of green for 70 feet to Clark St. It was a front lawn made to be the play place. When my parents moved there it was decided that the front yard would be the place to play. Their last home had a beautiful, big back yard, with swings and a garden and even a great tree for climbing. But without fail the boys always ended up in the front yard. It was where you wanted to be. You didn't want to miss out on other kids coming and going. It was the late 70's and that was what you did. You played with all the neighbor kids.

The lawn on Clark Street was lined by woods to the left and the driveway to the right. It's a gravel driveway in my mind. Mostly chalky dust still painful to walk on but worn so thin by the constant comings and goings of so many. It's probably been paved close to 20 years by now, but I've been gone for most of that.

It was the lawn where pictures were taken. In formal clothes or shoeless and ragged and smiling from joyful exertion and childhood exploring. It was the lawn we ignored from the porch while we ate breakfasts and read newspapers and chatted. The lawn we'd look out to on beautiful summer mornings, a thing not to be missed where I'm from, where snow is likely to cover the grass for 6 months solid, if not more, and laugh embarrassedly but lovingly as our parents would lie on the grass holding hands. Who knew what crazy things they were talking about, it wasn't the point at the time. The point was how weird our amazing and beautiful parents were. I could write those conversations now and while I'd be hard pressed for accuracy, I suspect they would read those words and hear the conversations they had, enjoying the privacy of their tiny Shangri-La in the middle of so much youthful burbling and angst. They'd have been telling each other the funny thing one of the kids said that the other hadn't heard. They'd be recounting the plans for the summer and making decisions while holding hands in the grass my mother liked to keep a little long and a little wild. They'd be living love the way you do when it surrounds you and consumes you and you find yourself awash in the logistics of simply maintaining such a healthy harvest. My father would have the chance to be funny. He was always funny. The quiet and opportunistic kind of funny. Observant and smart. The best funny, the kind that leads with the ear. But he'd get the chance to be funny for his lady. Funny in a way the kids wouldn't get and she couldn't resist. Before long, but not too quickly, life would remind them it's time to get back at it and they would. But they'd be back.

Across the street, a slow, unlined simple village road, was the park. It was Corbett Park but to us it was just the park. The park that watched us grow while it grew and changed over time. The park that had everything we ever needed, everything I ever needed. The park where we hid in order to explore being dangerous and being bad when we got older, where we could spend hours when we were little on now ancient seeming playground apparatus that our children will recoil at if they ever have kids of their own. Hardly believing that you could be spun so fast at 4 or 5 or 6 or older, depending on how big you were and how big the spinner was, so fast that you could hold on to the bars and with full extension spin endlessly. You'd fall and get up and try to swing so high that you'd be able to fully flip it. Never saw it, but I heard about it. We'd all heard about it.

When I got older the park became the basketball court for me, the parking lot for others. But during my prime people seemed to respect that the hoop on the Main Street side of the lot was mine and you parked on the far end. Or maybe it was just that way because for a good number of years I was out there, rain or shine, morning to night. When I was old enough I'd bring the car over and shoot in the lights with the radio on. It was my home court, always will be. I shoveled it to keep shooting. I would shoot in the middle of the night. Must have driven the neighbors crazy. All day every day. It was my first love. I always had basketball. Through ups and downs and joys and pains I always had that hoop.

When we wanted to test ourselves the park once again provided all we needed. At the back of the park, the horizon of that view from the small window at the kitchen sink, past the tennis courts was the pit. The pit was a giant hole dug at the back, between the park and the steep but small hill that led up to the towpath along the canal. It's fair to say we grew up between the Erie Canal and Lake Ontario, but we could walk to the canal, which we could see from our porch, in perhaps as much as 3 minutes while the lake was some twenty miles behind our house, through at least two other municipalities. Still, they were parameters of sorts, at least in my mind. Nothing that pinned us in, just something that gave us our bearings.

The pit would grow green like all the other open area in the flatlands that is the Great Lakes area of the country. But to us boys it was dirt. One solid line of dirt maybe a foot wide that started at the patch of trees that signified the point where the canal slope, the park and the pit convened. You'd disappear behind on your BMX bike as you'd gathered all the speed your legs and the descent from the towpath would get you. When you emerged from that tiny patch of trees you'd make another, shallow descent into the pit where you'd churn your legs as hard as you could. Maybe not that first time, but even then you'd fake it. Then you'd hit the best playground BMX jump that suburbia ever created and you'd soar, sometimes as much as 20 feet when you got good at it. I swear. It was epic.

To this day my mother says she was at the window in the kitchen when we proved it was a bad idea to do this kind of thing on a motorcycle. I say we, but it was one guy. He made it, but he also crashed through a chain link fence surrounding the tennis courts a good fifty feet from the lip of the jump. At least that's how I remember it. That's how we talk about it, which we do every couple of years now when it comes up.

At the end of the day you'd make your way home, walking up that long driveway and know how lucky you were. I can still sense it in every way just by closing my eyes. I can feel the gravel under my feet and smell the trees and the more subtle smell of long uncut grass. I can hear the birds making their nightly ascent from the woods we explored for thousands of hours. It's going to be one of the places I sense most vividly on my death bed no matter how old I am or how much I've lost. I love that big blue house on the middle of our block in a town I'll always love but I know I will see so rarely now that life is upon me and I'm busy trying to make a world half as magical for my kids to remember when they are out and finding what will be there home.

It may no longer be our house. It was our house and that's enough. Now there are other people making other memories and living the good life in the best place a kid could ever grow up. But in my heart and in my mind it will always be my house. The house I grew up in, the home I loved before all others. What a lucky kid I was.

Throwback Thursday, A Lifeline for Parents

A funny thing has happened to Facebook since you've been blessed with your babies. All those invisible friends who were having kids and obsessing over kids and posting pictures of their kids who were white noise to you before, they are now the people you notice and stop on as you scroll. The others with their pictures of drunken nights and play-house dinner parties in urban settings, dressed fashionably and looking for all the world like they are at a photo shoot are now cruelly taunting you as you hide on your toilet check in on the world through the window of your phone. It can feel awful. Look how much better everyone is doing then you. How fit and trim these other parents are and how interested they are in how their food is made and how much they can exercise. Which is strange because you are kind of, well, not totally, but yeah actually totally fat. Like fat in the face fat. Not just a little tight in the crotch fat, but all new pants and a new strategy at Kohl's kind of fat.

You aren't really aware that it's happened until you see a picture. But once you do see it, you know. You have crossed the line. It's gonna be a long journey to fitness.

You subsist largely on the three C's of early parenthood; candy, coffee and catnaps. Crying can be substituted for candy or catnaps. Coffee is untouchable. You are both dehydrated and bloated which seems impossible, but isn't. You are tired and sleepless and tasked with more than you knew you could do. So your glands seek sugar for the short bursts of energy you need. In this early phase with peeks of happiness driven by loving something more than you ever thought possible and lows of madness for exactly the same reason, you turn fat, grey and blobbish.

There is a light at the end of this tunnel. That light is hashtagged. #TBT. That's right. The mockable, thoroughly pleasurable social media phenomena of Throwback Thursday is your saving grace.

First, find all your friends whose kids are older than 8 and younger than college. Then, really wind yourself up by looking through their family photo albums. Look for albums with titles like, 'Fun Run 2013' or 'A Day at the Beach' or simply 'Mom Runs Two Marathons in One Week'. This should really get you to pull the trigger on those Donuts. Maybe even make you down a pint or two of Ben and Jerry's just before bed. You're not really searching the short energy burst at this point. Your just eating your feelings. It's a complicated emotional maneuver. Your recent trip through your closet, your truly fucked digestive system and your coworkers catching you wearing the only 2 pants you fit in anymore has led you to think there might be something to it.

Then do it. Find all those same friends with their grown kids and look at their various TBT photos of them with their babies at their first birthdays or first anything's, really. If they don't participate in TBT, no problem. Just scroll through their photos. You'll get there. You'll see the now dated photos of those parents, those marathoning sunbathers bundled in formless clothing, dressed perpetually for fall, playing with their babies, sprawled on couches and covered in kids. You'll see it. In addition to their beaming happiness and pride (they are after all curating these pics and they can only go so far in there unwitting role as caregiver to your broken psyche) you'll see the familiar pallor. The grey ghoul expression on their double chinned faces. Their general dishevelledness. You will see their wholly recognizable unwellness, and you will smile. They too were like you. They too lost all sense of self. There is hope that you may process food effectively again. You too may sleep and exercise and know the names of the movies, maybe even see a few, that were nominated this decade. There is a chance that you will once again order the flat fronts and not worry that your underbelly will be too evident.

There is hope.

What You Mean To Me

I write this blog to have a conversation with my kids that I need to have now. A conversation they can't yet join. I write it to put moments in a capsule. I put in as many as I can in hopes that some will reach moving targets at some far off time and provide some value to whomever it is that is interested enough to investigate this curiosity they've stumbled upon. My kids are the primary target, but their mother and I are also considered. We will likely be the first to come back to these words and pictures and visit our glorious past someday that's not nearly as far away as it was.

It can all disappear. It can happen in an instant or it can happen over time. What's certain, the only thing really, is that all of us will go away. Each and every one of us is renting. A hundred years from now, give or take, there will be all new tenants, each one deeply connected to the past from which they sprung, but each one also tied to a future we can't imagine. The slipperiness of it all is easy to understand and hard to truly fathom. What's promised to me is this minute. As such it seems important for me to try to truly explain to you both how much you mean to me.

You guys are my life's greatest achievement.

It's an entirely selfish assessment to be sure, but I have achieved things in life, everyone does, and truthfully, without question, whatever conceivable and inconceivable things that may yet come, you should know that I'll never ever do anything that will have meant more to me than raising you. What's silly is to think that theirs some list somewhere, even if it were to reside solely in my head, where there could possibly be something listed second. Nothing would deserve to be that close to you guys. Your mother feels the exact same way. From the second we met both of you we knew we had found our guiding stars, our purpose and our direction. I'm certainly still capable of making bad decisions, and sometimes I'll do things that will have some small negative effect on you. It's okay, we're all human and I hope you'll forgive me. What I know is my path is the one you're walking on in front of me. At times you'll drift and at times I will, but I know it will never be too far. I'll always walk that path behind you, keeping watch and marveling at your journey. At the paths you blaze as you make your way. It's been my life's greatest pleasure walking the path you've cut for me.

I'm so incredibly proud of you both.

It's insane to think that you'll have no frame of reference for what I mean when I'm saying it. After all you're 5 and 3 as I write this. You'll understand down the road. Truth is there's a little selfishness in this too. That's okay. Family relationships, the best ones, all the best ones contain certain aspects that would be hugely dysfunctional in all other relationships. Make no mistake, we are tied tight to you two. You'll wiggle free someday, even though we'll keep cinching and tugging, you'll break away. You should. Hell, I'll be proud of that too. Even through tears I'll be looking at your blurred silhouettes walking away as you must and I'll be filled with pride. Fear and love and anxiety and pride. It'll be right there with all the other feelings. Including lonely and perhaps a touch lost. But I'll be so proud. I'll also slip the rope through your belt loop and it will always be there ready for when you feel fully your own and want to come back and reminisce and learn what it was all about and who we were now that you've earned and learned a new perspective.

Language is insufficient to describe what you each mean to me.

I love you both to the ends of the earth. I love you past the ends of the earth. I love you across time and space and I love you in a way that the word love can't sufficiently convey.

When I was a kid I was cursed with parents who loved me. As a disaffected suburban youth this did not fit the narrative I was constructing and at times I rejected the love that was so generously heaped on me. It wasn't a jerk thing. I was just not aware of what my parents meant when they said they loved me. I didn't get that they were saying it not only to me but of me. They were expressing a thing that is far beyond what we know of love until we meet our kids. Perhaps others find it elsewhere than with children, perhaps you will. For my life, for my parent's lives it was becoming parents. I can no longer speak to any other experience than the one where I become a parent and I can tell you that I'm so very much in love with the life it's given me. The life you've given me. Sure, there are no doubt times when the business of parenting could best be classified as my favorite frustration. What's interesting about that is that in retrospect it all turns into beauty, even the parts that might feel awful to live through.

I'm planning a long adventure that takes us all down the path as far as we can go together. I'm aware that we won't all be on the path together forever. But I'm also aware that we will be on that path, together, forever. Because whatever else may be happening and whenever you may be reading this you should know, the minute you guys came along you removed all the boundaries that I had assigned to myself. You stretched that moment to the length of a lifetime and proceeded to teach me how to dance on it, free of the burdens I'd imagined weighed so heavy before you taught me to let them go. You are the magic that makes my life complexly beautiful and you brought with you all the joy and love to last a thousand lifetimes.

We're not promised tomorrow, but we have today. I'm so happy to be here with you two.

Rantings of a Middle Aged Dad

I get it. It's a different time. We aren't as connected and our lives intersect virtually rather than physically. No longer is the fabric weaved tightly enough to allow for our children to roam safely upon it.

Lately there's a certain level of mental and perhaps spiritual health and wellbeing that I can only achieve by waving a clenched fist in the air and flapping my gums about whatever it is that bugs me. I'm entering the 'get off my lawn' stage of life. These are my greying and grumpy years. In an effort to get through this quite annoying phase I am attempting to yell my displeasure into the void that once was a neighborhood as I stand on my porch in my slippered feet and ever expanding belly, fueled by fear and confusion just as eons of men have done before me. I'm not afraid to be a stereotype.

What the hell is wrong with people?

Why is everyone so damn angry? Why is everyone in love with those of us most boldly expressing free floating rage with the least responsibility and the greatest amount of hostility? When did we adults become so fragile, kicking and screaming when things don't go exactly as we want them to? I feel like my grandparents generation rolled with the punches so much better. They understood that your vote was your voice and when more people voted for the other guy you had to accept it. Nowadays, disguised in tough guy individualism, everyone's a bunch of ninnies outraged that the world is not there to serve them solely, exactly meeting the very specific needs of precisely one person. 300 million 'one person's', all dissatisfied and lashing out. Grownups ain't what they used to be.

Superheroes are for kids!

Grow up!

Don't get me wrong. I'm not impugning the quality of those films that get it right. Good films are good films, regardless of genre. You can tell a good story about anything. But superheroes now are terrifying, angry, violent and often vile. They live in a world that looks like ours if you did nothing but look at it via cable news and clickbait terrors all day. Then they are marketed to 2 and 3 year old's who suddenly want even their stuffed Elmo's and Winnie the Pooh's to 'battle'! Call me crazy, but hidden documents will emerge that show the companies that underpin the military-industrial complex were huge supporters of this simple way to desensitize humanity to constant 'battle' or war as us old timers used to call it.

Honestly, had I known I'd have treated superheroes like alcohol. Not until you are of legal age and your hormones have settled a bit.

College is a vitally important scam that I have to participate in to better the odds that my children can earn enough to barely get by.

Seriously. What a crock.

My parents' generation was the last to not leave college in massive debt. State schools are running in the tens of thousands per year now. What the actual bleep is that? More and more it feels like the systems are established to make sure that only those that can find a way to pay the toll are allowed to get through the eye of the needle that will allow them to get a job that will overwork and underpay them to keep them on the treadmill as long as possible. And these, these are the lucky ones! I left college with a worthless degree and 25K in debt, which is a DREAM scenario for my own kids at this point.

Fix it! This is unsustainable, unethical and unbelievable.

We have legalized drug dealing and it's taking over your television.

Have you seen the lines at the pharmacy in the last 15 years? Of course you have. You have stood in them, just like I have. We are over served. Somebody needs to start giving us sugar pills and sending us home to sober up.

There are a ton of reasons why I can't watch commercial TV with my kids. The lewd lasciviousness of the content is tame next to the practically pornographic nature of those commercials that aren't verging on actual depictions of evil. But for god's sake, don't make me have to sit there watching you push drugs for everything imaginable. Recently I've started seeing commercials for drugs that help offset the side effects of OTHER DRUGS! What the hell!

Have some shame people. Racism, sexism and xenophobia is reprehensible not electable.

Donald Trump. Donald freaking Trump. You did this to yourselves. I've had enough of the lot of you.

GET THE HELL OFF MY LAWN!

If You're Gay...

You two keep us delightfully, exhaustively, sometimes even maddeningly busy. In the future, a thing that when I was a kid we thought of as 20-30 -40 years hence, but a thing that appears to be forever a year away in this time of ever evolving technology, I hope to be able to keep up better with the details of the news. For now I get what I get through imperfect routes to be sure. It's hard to filter through for what information is important for me to know.

What's coming through right now is that voices of hate that hope to marginalize and demonize those that are different seem to be growing bold with the increasing wind of public support. Fear not, there are countervailing winds that are stronger, winds that I hope you'll join us in generating as you grow up and encounter a world of rich and beautiful diversity. I hope you'll try to recognize all that you have and be appreciative.

You have parents that likely won't be able to send you wherever you want to go for college and won't have you in a new car on your sixteenth birthday. We live knowing that the plenty we have is merely where we need to put our resources for now as what's most important to us is you guys and your wellbeing. We wish we could give you everything you ever wanted, but we know we will never be able to. We see value in that as well.

What we can give you we give easily and freely and it's us, all of us and all the love we contain. It's our greatest pleasure giving it to you and these are our golden years as you have not ever thought of withholding it from us. Any contentiousness that might rise between us at your young ages is gone before it could ever settle in and turn into a thing that might feel permanent.

Truth is its normal, at least to some degree, to have tense times with your parents as you grow up. You are duty bound to become independent and as much as we want that for you we are equally compelled to hold on to you for as long as possible. The love we feel for you is overwhelming and we can't let go. There's perhaps a fear of mortality thing involved here as well, I'm starting to sense. Whatever it is, you'll be ready to get out in the world and make your mistakes and learn how to regroup and make them again, as many times as you need to, well before we'll feel comfortable letting you. I bring it up now because from here, driving toward the fire, I have my wits about me. It seems a lot harder to maintain such perspective, seeing the fire as a controlled burn, one that makes the land it decimates capable of sustaining new life as it comes closer. I'm pretty sure it won't feel that way when I'm standing in the fire trying to keep you from running in, where all the action is, where all the pain and excitement are that I'm projecting onto you, er, the fire.

I'm losing the analogy. Suffice it to say that the teen and young adult years can be hard on everyone. You are all better for getting through them, but it's possible for us to lose one another there for a bit.

And what a bit it is. Your teen years are amazing. If they're anything like mine they will contain Odyssey's that you will look back on with great fondness, experienced with comrades taking similar though specifically different journeys all of which I'm happy to have behind me and don't want to go back to.

There is a fear that I have that I can't shake and I want to make sure, just in case this is a place where you ever find me, to address it.

I love you. I want you to find and feel loved. I want you to know that love is what I want for you most. I want you to know that you deserve to feel loved and to love. What I don't care about is who you find it with, not the demographics of them at least. I certainly want that person to respect you. I will be over the moon if they make you laugh. They should definitely inspire your curiosity. I want you to find love with someone that challenges you to grow and takes unexpected journeys with you. I want you to be that person that sparks a fire for someone else.

Who's to say what they future holds. I didn't find that person, your mom, until much later than many others do. You're five and three and today I saw pictures of my prom dates kids going to prom. It took me a while, but I'm glad I didn't stop looking. That said, if your love becomes your work or your family or your boundless thirst for experience and adventure or if you find it in stacks of books or making music or walking in the woods, I don't care, as long as it makes you happy.

And if you find love with a wife and you have a life that looks like ours, with kids and a yard and walking to school and it's filled with love, I'll be delighted.

And if you fall in love with a man and you spark and you make a life filled with love, and laughter and experiences that make you feel the world was made just for you, just like this life feels for me, you will find no one in the world more delighted and happy for you than me.

I need you to know because it all emerges at a time, the teen years, when we feel most alone and despite a world, a country that still insists on retracting the progress that is so hardly won for tolerance and acceptance and love please know that I'm for you and will be so proudly and loudly. Whoever you are, whoever you love.

My Kodachromatic Memories

I've had tightness in my chest and shallow breathing for going on a month. It's largely a result of pollen and my body's late life decision to no longer recognize that springtime friend that greeted me with joy for so many years as I thawed out from so many winters. What was once my friend, the dawning of life in the blooming and bursting nature outside my door is now my enemy, a predator and my body has chosen, without consulting me, to fight it using all the parts of me I can't control as its shield.

It's no big deal. It's a minor pain in the ass that I forget about sometime in May and remember in early spring annually. The older I get the less invincible I am.

I'm changing jobs and as exciting as it is I'm taking on a massive new challenge. I'm looking forward to it and I'm thinking about it and the tightness in my chest feels a natural psychosomatic reaction as well. Though I know it isn't. It's merely my body deciding not to work like it once did. Same way the knees did when I tried to run the Brooklyn half 10 or more years ago. I made it one mile before hobbling to a train and turning to low impact elliptical's in the gym. The way my lithe and supple and strong body turned to a big and broad and strong body before turning to a big and unresponsive mass. Thankfully I'm told the heart keeps getting stronger even if it's harder and harder to make what I see in the mirror reflect what I still think I am in my brain.

Getting older is hard for many reasons. The physical reasons are a lot to be sure and I've only just begun that journey. Being where I am now, mid-career, early family and years from financial security is a constant struggle. The same one so many travel with me. But there are also the dawning realizations that an active mind, one at rest and given a few minutes to contemplate can't help but notice. For me it can happen in the car or at work or watching my kids in the back yard as they bounce from one thing to the next, bound by no laws of energy I've come to think of as universal since being bound by them years ago. It's all gonna end and it's gonna happen soon.

I love my kids beyond all reason. It's the only way I know how to do it at this point. I understand that there are some terrible situations out there where children aren't afforded that type of love and it shatters me when I hear of bad things, scary things happening to them. Things I could watch in movies or read about in the news years ago about terrible things happening to young children are no longer things I can ignore. I feel it now viscerally. It kills me now in a way it never could have before. It's empathy for strangers and it's hard to have at times, but it's proof to me of some sort of reason for all this. My mind intellectualizes and thinks that reason is survival, we are here and our point is to survive. Even if that's so, for me that contains within it what others find in God.

I'm a slightly older dad, but in a life so short as this one even slightly older has ramifications. Perhaps nostalgia just overtakes you at this age, I don't know. What I know is that for me the overwhelming rush to nostalgia and the amplifying emotional response to it is something that came around the same time I had kids. In a real way they've been my greatest teachers about what life is all about. I'm living in a museum at this point. Our home is awash in the memories that will be those I sprint to as the 'time of my life.' This is the golden passage that will live longest in my mind, this time when we are a small, highly interdependent family whose only plans, only one's we can even imagine, revolve around all of us. Their will come a time when that isn't so, which is sad to think about.

All the stuff to come actually has some sadness in it. For me at least. Because what's next after our family is our slow walk away. We aren't going to live forever. Even those of you firmly in belief that this is not it, that there is more after, surely even you must share some of the melancholy I can have when it hits me that what comes next isn't this. This amazing life all opened up to me, when my kids want to hug me and read with me and kiss me and tell me they love me.

For me it's good to remember that I'm going to die. It's a positive reminder that what we don't take and hold and cherish will be gone. Nostalgia is my guide as I look longingly back at the life I've lead to here and all that life yet to happen, yet to be stored in memory. We curate this museum in our minds, Karen and I. We arrange and rearrange the memories because we simply love to hold them. In doing so I've come to learn the value of my young memories.

In those memories of my youth the world is colored like 70's and 80's quality Kodak film and there are faded edges. My mother is there in her Jean bandana and my dad in t-shirt and Lee's and we're eating cereal from little boxes at picnic tables at Hamlin Beach, about fifteen miles from home. They had six kids and it was how we took some vacations. We loved them. Or we're at Hershey park and loving the rides and smelling chocolate in the air. Or we're all crammed into any of a series of station wagons driving down the highway on our way to adventures. I'm sitting in the back facing bench seat, crouched so my back is where my butt should be, so I can dangle my bare feet out the rear window, dangling in the Kodachromatic sun as the wind sweeps over the lot of us from all the open windows, always open in the summer, a thing we barely do anymore.

I have to visit there to keep my mom mommy and to see my dad as the strapping man much younger than I am now managing what I now am able to see was a circus of nonstop work, that I lived in and couldn't possibly conceive of then. I have to go back there to keep the edges from fading in any further than they already have. These are the glory times of my life, just like these times are now, and for the rest of time I'll return there, here, because I don't want to go.

Life can only be lived forward and as far as I can tell it can only be lived once which is its only flaw. I used to think nostalgia was something silly people did who were afraid of life but I was dead wrong. It's what lucky people do to remember all that was so graciously and gloriously bestowed on them.

I Don't Want To Let Go

Teddy still babbles. He'll sit with the Lego Duplo's and play by himself and there is a stream of playful and emotive gibberish. He has started to use words and pretend and play make believe with his creations and the figurines, but if I listen in the right way, if I'm able to listen loosely I can still hear the patter of the 2 year old he was.

Being a parent is a lot. Early on we weren't up to the task. Seriously. We are excellent, loving parents. Any kid, and I mean any kid at all would be lucky to have us. But the truth is that as excellent as we are as parents, we just aren't very good at it. We don't revert naturally to routine. We don't always provide excellent examples and we are just terrible at doing so many of the things that we are 'supposed' to do.

Our house is a mess and while it's better than it was, it's never gonna be an ordered and soothing environment. I like to think that has to do with our artistic bent, that our clutter and struggle to eliminate is an element of us that is strongly informed by our connectedness and the meaning we see all around us. Meaning that I turn into stories.

We don't sleep train. We shouldn't have to at this point, frankly. Our kids are well past the age when that should not be a thing that needs doing. I'm afraid that if our kids are ever to get themselves to bed, it's gonna happen on its own. For now we each take one and we snuggle and struggle and ultimately find them asleep sometime within a couple hours of getting them up the stairs and into their rooms. In my case, with the three year old it is sometimes in the chair after losing the fight of getting him to calm down in his bed. Other times it is both of us on the floor looking up at the green stars on the ceiling that emanate from Winnie's honey pot when you press the bee. Sometimes we find the moon, other times we find the one constellation, an outline of Mickey Mouse's head. Yep, Disney even invades their sleep. Still other times it's on the 'big boy bed' the five year old will be moved to once I am able to solve this endlessly flummoxing Rubik's Cube of a task that I am told should never have been allowed to get to this point. In my moments of confidence, a wonderful if fleeting thing when it comes to my life as a dad, I like to think that whatever we're losing by not giving them normalized sleep routines is more than made up for by the love and feeling of security we're giving them by never leaving.

We are inconsistent practitioners of reward systems, a crime doubly indictable as I've been designing and implementing such programs for much of my 20+ year career. We don't practice anything approaching appropriate self-care. The clothes are piled up, usually separated into piles that require sniff tests to determine whether they are clean or dirty. We take them into our bed and let them stay the night. Every time. We are wonderful parents to have as we never fail to give love. But we are just not very good at the component skills.

I'm not complaining. Well, not much. Now that our lives are this way I can honestly say there's very little I would change. Perhaps I'd employ more consistent rewards or maybe I'd have a few more date nights. I'd certainly have a neater pile of clutter, that's for sure. Okay, there's a lot I'd change.

But I won't, because at this point, this is who we are. We are fumbling through this thing together, imperfect as hell. I'm not saying we refuse to grow or we won't change. We're changing all the time, growing all the time. We're just doing it together. At this point that means we're messy, tired, together and happy.

I don't know how much longer I'm going to be able to hear through the coherent play and listen to the babbling that is working its way fully out of my son's mouth. Truth is I might already have heard the last of it. That's the thing. Nothing we do is going to stop them from growing up. Nothing I do will keep us from watching life slip ever past. The older they get and the older we get the more clear it becomes that none of it is forever. None of it lasts like I'd like it to.

It kills me to think that I'm ever going to step out, I'm ever going to be finished. With loving and watching and helping and messing up with my kids. That I'm ever going to walk away from my wife who I'll never see again or that she'll have to walk away from me. I don't want any of this to change because for the first time since I was too young to understand the implications of it, I don't want to ever die.

I want to live forever and never say goodbye. Never grow old. Never die. I want to live this life I have for a million lifetimes. Not some version of it, not some other life, but this one. Mine. With the same pains and the same joys. Now every day that goes by where I don't hear my boy babble, like the ones that came before he uttered a sound and relied on us for his every aspect of existence, every tiny change that moves some aspect of their lives to the past is a process. One of letting go. That is how we think of it.

I often think that parenthood is the first time it's highlighted for you that so much of life is the process of constantly letting go. It is, but it also isn't. It gives me some agency, some power, some sense that this is my choice. To let go. To slowly choose to hand away life one tiny handful at a time, knowing that at the end the last thing I'll let go of will be life itself. It's inevitable. It'll be all I have left to hand over.

That's not how it is though, is it? I don't want to let any of it pass. I want to live equally in the moments where I was three, sitting on my momma's lap playing with her long hair that flowed out of her '70's style bandana, staring at the wooden cross hanging from a leather strap around her neck. I want to spend eternity smiling at the brown lunch bag my father drew pictures on just for me. I want to fall in love for the first time at 12 years old and play act what I thought it meant to lose it all. I want to feel lean and limber and strong and beautiful as I dance with a basketball unafraid of anyone who might wish to stop me. I want to be brash and cocky and altogether terrified on my first day of college and I want the world to open up to me at camp as I found what it was I'd do the rest of my life. I want to meet my wife, sit on those bar stools forever. Falling in love and diving into the unknown. I want to have my kids, meet them for the first time, and I want to watch them grow and marvel at the spectacle. I want all of this to be held. Why would I ever let go of this?

The answer is obvious. We 'let go' because we have no choice. Because we can't choose to hold on. That being said, I want to get as much of this as I can. I want to watch my boy play on the floor with not a care in the world but what the little elephant on the back of his train that he built from Lego's and imagination is going to do next. Forever.

My Father Gave Me Love and Art

The home I grew up in, the one I'll only see in pictures and inhabit only behind my closed eyes ever again, was one that had life oozing, sometimes tumbling, out of every corner and on every wall. Hell, the walls themselves can never fully mean to someone else what they meant to us. You see, my father is an artist and he designed our home. He'll hasten to point out that he's a designer, and he'd of course be right. But art is in the eye of the beholder. In fact I'd use a version of his own argument against him if he ever were to push back too hard. Not that he would, I suspect. He's always been a dad that's happy to allow us to be wrong and to learn in our own time. As we've gotten older and wiser the times that time has proven us right have increased and on this one I'm right. Just like he was when someone would say that Norman Rockwell was not an artist, but rather an illustrator. Besides, my dad's art, much of it from his 'art school' days, some from the days when they were a young couple trying to decorate a home, hung all over those walls he designed.

Now 'illustrator', at least as far as I can tell, holds no innately pejorative meaning. It's not an insult to call someone who illustrates an illustrator. But in the particular case of an artist of Mr. Rockwell's talent and the way in which his work was received by so many contemporaries and more recently by so many subsequently, there is no mistaking the pejorative if not downright disdainful way the term 'Illustrator' is spit out in regard to this man's considerable work. Now I paraphrase here, and my dad is not one given to high emotion, but I'm quite certain that my father would find this assessment to be straight up baloney. Or Bologna, if you prefer. It rankled him. His art was no less artful for being purchased. Was in fact far more technically impressive, emotive and often breathtaking than the celebrated works of his contemporaries who looked to shock or amuse rather than paint and convey. I believe these things. I did even at my most harshly judgmental, Brooklyn bohemian, cravenly desirous of the approval of the cool people that I ever was. Because my dad was right.

We went out of the way for a day on a family vacation when we were kids to spend a night in Stockbridge so we could visit the Rockwell museum and the work is extraordinary. I assume we stayed *near Stockbridge.* Even then it was ridiculously expensive and we were a family of 6-9 kids, depending on when you caught us. I mean, I have

2 and we're challenged to make a day at the beach. But my dad, he was going to see the Rockwell Museum, and we were going to as well.

The art that hung on our walls, it was and is beautiful. It was original and creative and something I'll have a sense memory of until the day I die. There were pieces made of crepe paper and lacquer, some evoking scenes from nature others crinkled and crumpled and exploding from the frame out to you. As a kid, even now I'm sure, I'd be hard pressed to resist feeling them, running my hands over the points and crevices, riding the ridges of the bright orange that has never seemed to fade with time. Or the hard wood drawn on with varying sized nails hammered in that should seem hard and unforgiving but convey soft fluidity as the lines denote structure and movement from top to bottom. The figure could be wind, it could be human, it could be a spirit. I could look forever and for me it would never fully be decided. Or the dark stained blocks, different shapes and sizes, but all right angles, creating a skyline if laid flat, and a sense of looking down on a city as they hung in their frame on the wall.

Art wasn't just something he did. He breathed art. There was something of it in the very life he'd crafted. He is 6'3" and as a young man, for at least the first 15 or 16 years of my life he had a big, bushy black beard. He looked, as EVERYONE noted, like a living, breathing Abraham Lincoln.

He and his beautiful, loving wife had 6 kids. They didn't always have enough to make it all work, but somehow they did. Didn't matter, even if they couldn't, there was always room for one more at the table. Anyone who knew us, even just a little, they always knew that about them. Many would ascribe it to my mother, a truly charitable and loving soul, but they were a team. The decisions they made were based on what served the greater good, what completed their vision of what a beautiful life looked like. For my father that picture was one that couldn't avoid including art and curiosity, and daydreaming and all that it had given his life. He was a designer, true, but he was an artist not only of multiple media's when that term meant something altogether different.

Art was a living and breathing thing in our home. I don't know that this part is true, but I even think that my dad's parents met somehow through community theater. This may be a fanciful fiction, but it's got some truth in it, even if it isn't fully 'correct.' Music, books, theater, these were all an integral part of life growing up in the Medler home. I wasn't quite brave enough to try to participate in the creation of said art like my older brothers were when I was a kid, but I sure am happy I was exposed to it. I became a big reader and lover of novels. It was what spoke to me. They were performers. I envied them. I'm glad I've found and stuck to writing. I'm glad to be a part of this part of the family legacy in some small way, even if it doesn't exactly mesh with the rest.

My father also communicated with me through art. When I was not much older than ten, maybe twelve, we found ourselves home alone for an evening. Honestly, I'm the third child in a family of six, or sixth of nine if you choose to define our family in the most inclusive way, as we all do, and this might be the only time when we found ourselves in this predicament. My younger sisters were at friends' houses, my youngest brother may have been traveling with my mom, or maybe he was not even born yet, I'm not sure. In any case, I distinctly remember my father mentioning that he'd heard an interview earlier in the day and that Pete Seeger and Arlo Guthrie were playing at Finger Lakes that night. He really wished he could have gone.

'Why don't we go?' I said. I knew Arlo Guthrie was the guy who did the Alice's Restaurant song. I liked that.

'Yeah?' He asked.

'Yeah.' I said. I was really excited. Things like this had yet to start happening for me.

That night we just drove out there and stayed for the whole thing. It was great. My first concert. Pete Seeger and Arlo Guthrie with my dad. A night to remember indeed. He even played Alice's Restaurant and his shtick was pretty amusing. I had no idea how much of an inspiration Pete Seeger would become as I grew up. He seemed super old then and I don't think he'd even STARTED cleaning the Hudson yet, though I'm certain I'm way off. I didn't know he had, anyway.

Another time he rented Breaking Away from Wegman's on a Friday night and said, 'you should watch this. It's important.' He would later rent Brazil and say I should check it out. Wasn't of any use though as neither of us could make any sense of it.

In our home, filled with art, there was a piece of furniture that no longer seems to hold the place of importance it once did as a family focal point. Our Stereo. It was six feet long, two and a half feet tall and big. Speakers covered in earth tone fabric occupied either end in full and in the middle was a door that rolled open. Behind it were the records that were important enough to keep out, to listen to. Eventually we'd overrun his truly beautiful collection with Disco Duck and K-Tel Collections, but early on, it was magical. All the first editions of the Beatles, Beach Boys, Ray Charles. My father's favorite band, The Lovin' Spoonful. I remember dancing in underoos to 'Summer in the City.' Loving the Beatles before knowing it was a band anyone other than us knew. I remember my seventh birthday and my cool cousin buying me 'Off the Wall' after seeing how much I loved every time 'Don't Stop Til You

Get Enough' came on and having something that could stay in the Stereo. It felt so SO grown up. I had taste, I had arrived, I had something adult enough to have to stay in the stereo when the doors rolled closed. Now my music, my history in songs largely stays in my pocket, on my phone. I'm sure it will seep out and as they get older more and more music will return to the air. But it'll never hold the mystique and the mystery and the excitement that the stereo in the shape of an upright freezer in the dining room held.

My father has given me more than I could ever possibly recall. He gave me life, after all. As a father now I realize that even more than that, he gave us, all of us, his life. Freely and fully and happily. I'm endlessly thankful for it. But beyond that, beyond the sacrifice and the work and the love he also gave me art and I can't thank him enough for that.

Deliberate Diversity: A Family Story

My mother's birthday was last week. I've been thinking about her a lot lately. I've been remembering a story she once told me. I'm fuzzy on the details but I'll do my best.

She was a young girl of about 17 when one of the nuns scheduled a meeting with her in her office. This was at my mother's school, Notre Dame Academy. It was a new world and there were new conversations that needed having. I'm sure for my mother, young and brave and unafraid, it was no big deal. I'm not sure how prepared these nuns were to advise these young women, however, about entering a world that was evidently and obviously changing while they were largely committed to persevering in their calling.

Regardless, it was the good sister's job to have a counseling session with the young ladies in her charge to discuss each girl's future plans. It was right around the landing of the Beatles at Idlewild and performing on Ed Sullivan and what changes were coming could hardly be predicted. What was evident however was that young women had options. So the meetings were designed as an opportunity to ask these girls what it was they intended to do upon graduating. They were discussions that perhaps were designed to elicit answers of no real variation from the choices that were laid out for young women prior to this time, asked by folks who expected girls to hew to the norm, to lean in to 'safe' and to impose on themselves the restrictive, narrow set of options that had been thrust upon their moms and grandmothers. Surely they assumed this exercise would teach these girls that any ideas of rebellion were silly and not to be bothered with. Well, as is often the case when asking what one thinks to people who haven't been solicited before, surprise abounds.

So few would answer in ways that the nuns expected. I can't imagine what they thought when the plans included anything beyond teaching of small children, secretary school, nursing or looking to marry and have children. Surely many would still want some of these things, but many didn't. My mom was somewhere in between.

'Barbara. It's nothing to be afraid of. I've known you for years now and I know who you are and whatever you are thinking will surely be less alarming to me than you can possibly imagine. Allow me to assure you, your answer will not be the most shocking one I've received. Now please, tell me what you imagine your life will be. What do you intend to do after leaving school?', asked the good sister.

My mother, a decidedly 'good' kid, wasn't afraid at all that she would shock her interviewer. She might surprise her, sure. Her concern was that she would tell her it was impossible. She would tell her she was silly for having such a dream, such a vision for a life.

'I'm sure I'll go to secretary school. The one in the city.' She replied, avoiding eye contact.

'Yes, Barbara, you've said. What do you intend to do with your life. You can't be a secretary forever.'

To be fair to my mom, these questions weren't really answerable. She was seventeen(ish) and her plans for what she'd do ten steps down the road were as unknowable as they were unlikely to turn out true. Still, she had an answer and at this point it was a power struggle. After fighting her way through the interviews with the girls who dreamed of marrying floppy haired British musicians and others that thought they could run entire companies or fly airplanes or do whatever it was they had gotten into their heads, well, Sister was not going to let Barbie Monohan skate by without engaging.

'Tell me, Barbara. What is there to be afraid of?' She asked.

'You'll think me silly.'

'I will not.'

'You will. And you'll tell me it's a fantasy and not a plan.'

'We'll see if you are right only when you tell me.'

So my mother, having developed a touch of the courage, answered the good sister.

'I'm going to have a family. A huge family, with 12 children. They will be of every color and from all over the world. I want to be a mother to a rainbow of god's children.' She said.

Well. She was right, thought the good sister. That is silly.

'Barbara, I don't think you understood the question. Are you even dating someone?'

'I did understand your question and no, I'm not dating anyone. You want to know what I intend to do. My answer is that I plan to have a big family filled with children of all colors, I want to be a mother to a rainbow of God's children.'

After some serious scowling, a few more attempts to knock her back on course, the sister dismissed my determined mother. From the room and from her head. She dismissed her as a silly girl who didn't know anything and still imagined fairy tales were real. She dismissed her as someone who had a lot to learn.

She dismissed her wrongly.

My mother ended up with a big, diverse, multicultural, multiracial house full of children. She stayed open to her hope coming true and woke years later exhausted, exuberant and with the life she could see that no one around her could have fathomed.

We were an odd lot in the pew. Six tall kids with complexions that reflected our (very) Northern European heritage, two black boys (if it was summer and D was up) and a teenage girl from Vietnam. We rolled nine deep, with at least 4 different heritages and at minimum 4, if not more, colors on the rainbow of god's children. Perhaps it wasn't an honest to goodness Roy G. Biv rainbow, but it was a pretty damned great approximation of a youthful dream.

I don't know what's happening in our world. I've been writing a lot about race relations for the past year or two. Sadly a great many reasons have kept it at the top of my mind. The most recent tragedies come in the midst of a public conversation that no longer seems to adhere to the rules of decency that at least kept the truly ugly stuff behind closed doors. I'm of two minds about this. On the one hand allowing the truly awful, secret hatred to be spewed out allows us to have the conversation. Compels us to acknowledge realities many of us have been able to ignore for far too long and in the end perhaps these conversations being had in the light of day instead of behind millions of closed doors will ultimately help us evolve and truly change. On the other hand hate has never had such cache in our communal discourse and it's getting to where you can hardly avoid it. How can this be good? How can we ever hope to change when the truly ignorant are empowered by the truly powerful indulging in hateful, small minded, shameless racism and brazen sexism?

My children live in a diverse world, to some degree. There are kids at their daycare of many shades and backgrounds. That said, it's not as diverse as my house was growing up. We have family over for birthday parties, uniformly white family. The kids on our block are largely white as are the kids we saw at the kindergarten orientation that Charlie went to a few months back. I worry about how we got here. The schools were literally ranked first in the state when we found the house and that's the main point of conversation we had around whether the town was a good place to grow up. Diversity didn't come up in any real way. It wasn't a part of the calculus.

I don't know how my mom did it. I should note clearly at this point that she did not do it alone. My dad was of course steering the ship as well, but to some degree, just based on how everyone arrived at our house, it was a function of my mom. She's a much more social being than either my father or I. Or really most people you'll come across. It was her relationships as far as I can tell that diversified our world. Many of her friends were different looking than her. If there was an organizing principle it was faith, but even that was diverse.

My mother wanted to see a different kind of church and in doing so met a mentor and friend, Algerene. Algerene was a foster mother to dozens over the years, a committed and hardworking, and an incredibly gifted servant of her faith, not to mention a gourmet Chef. My mother met her when she had the opportunity to cross lines and go to the church where she stuck out as the 'other'.

On a very sad day, the day we buried Algerene's son, my brother, John, another brother, D, was at the house as we celebrated his life after a service where so many tears were shed. Well, John had an older brother, I believe he lived in Chicago and he wasn't a huge part of John's adult or even teen life, but he was of course there for this. Well, when D introduced himself he did so by saying, 'Yeah, you ever get pictures from John. Yeah, well, I'm the other ink spot in the milk bowl.' Funny and true. Well, in the church where she met Algerene my mother would have been the milk spot in the ink bowl. She did that. She was curious so she went. Didn't think twice about it. Didn't think it particularly notable. She was curious so she went. In the end she made a dear, lifelong friend. For a number of reasons that friend had a son that moved in with us and stayed.

D is another story. Without going into all the details, from what I know D came up for the summers through a program that paired city kids with non-city families. We were that non-city family. The program ran for years. Maybe 5 or six. We'd always schedule our vacations around when he was gonna be there. Turns out the first couple years he was nervous around my mom. When she finally asked him why he said it was because every time he showed up the baby had a black eye. I was that baby and I liked to fall on things at a very early age apparently. The story is good for a laugh now that it's long ago as my mother is gentler than anyone you've ever known. In the end my parents kept bringing D up for summers on their own accord after the program expired. When D was looking to finish his studies he came back to live with us. He's been up there ever since.

Our vacations were always in the camper. My dad drove the wagon and we all loaded into it and drove and drove until we got to where we were going. We went to campgrounds, amusement parks, Baseball's Hall of Fame... We got everywhere with that thing in those early years. It wasn't until years later that I found out that one of those trips when we had the adventure of staying in the trailer it was because those folks we were visiting weren't comfortable with the makeup of our family. My mom and dad could have chosen to take vacation at a different time. We could have been more 'acceptable'. They didn't do that. We stayed in the driveway and had our wonderful visit and some ideas might even have gotten changed in the time we were there. No big deal was made about it. Only figured it out as an adult.

My sister, who is Vietnamese, let's call her May, came to live with us when I was five and not ready to have another person to compete for attention with. I'm afraid I may not have been that nice to her when I was very little. But all that was behind us when I was 16. That was when we all loaded up in the minivan and made our way to King of Prussia in Pa. That was where May was marrying a young Vietnamese man she met at school.

May is amongst the strongest people I can imagine. Her story is hers and I would never relay it, but it speaks to a person who had to be stronger than I ever imagine I'll ever have to be. When we were asked to be in her wedding, well, snot nose that I was, I said no. I feel terrible about that. I said I didn't want to wear a tux. I don't know what that was about. Thankfully my brothers are loving and kind and caring and were happy to be ushers. The plan was for my dad to walk May down the aisle and give her away. It was going to be beautiful. Well, as it turns out, May's family of origin, who she hadn't seen on over a decade, were granted visas and were going to make it to the States in time for the wedding.

I remember it being a late afternoon wedding and my parents taking us all, dressed up, to a McDonald's on the way. It was going to be a while until dinner and it was going to be all Vietnamese food and we were a family of at least 6 at that time, 6 kids that is. They had to do something to ensure we didn't starve. Then we went to the wedding. I felt terrible for my silly stance and wished I was there next to my big brother helping guests to their seats. I might have even asked if I could, but I probably didn't.

What happened in that wedding was beautiful to me and still is to this day. My dad, May's American dad, walked her down the aisle, stopped at the front pew, and released her where her dad who hadn't seen her grow up from a young girl to the young woman she was now, but who moved heaven and earth to get back to her, took her the rest of the way to 'give her away'. Like watching the movie Glory, or speaking in public about acts of selflessness or my family, whenever I tell this part of the story it makes me well up and brings me close to crying.

I don't think my parents would ever say they were intentional about being inclusive. They would never think to. If you asked them they might say yes, but it wouldn't cross their minds to think about it. But they were. They were intentional. Right from the time my mother told that Nun that she wished it, there was intent to be inclusive. To integrate their lives.

I want to give my kids the same experience. A life soaked in differing perspectives unified by the common thread of shared experience. I want them to know that differences are to be celebrated. That seeing someone that may appear slightly differently, who might speak another language or have different traditions is nothing to be threatened by, but rather is something to feel excited about.

I can't say that I'm without bias. I can fully say that I want to be. I can say that if I'm ever to catch myself I immediately, consciously work to alleviate bias. I fear that the events that have transpired are the result of segregation. I worry that we as Americans, as white Americans have come too easily to accept that this separation of large parts of us is due to organically occurring circumstances and that we shouldn't think about it. That if people wanted to move in next door and go to the same schools as our kids and live in the same town as us all they'd have to do is choose to do so. We have well maintained roads, good schools, ample security and we assume it is the same for those in areas we choose not to live in.

It's not true. No less than Newt Gingrich, scion of the Republican revolution said as much. He said that after long conversations, ones where he acknowledged he was not informed and in which he had, for a long time denied the reality that he now was sharing. That white Americans, many of us, can't possibly know what it's like to be black in America.

It's hard to see what you aren't exposed to. It would be nice if the default that we all fell to was empathy. It would be nice if we all reverted to a position of identifying with the despair of others. We've all felt despair. But it's starting to be made clear that is not where we default to. Not all of us. When confronted with these humans, these people who have different pigmentation, some of us see first with minds that are fueled by fear. Fear of the different. Fear of the unknown. Fear of the other.

I don't want this for my children. I don't want this for their friends. I don't want this for children and friends having a different experience than ours. I want so badly to be intentional about diversity. But I am failing.

Of all people, I should know better.

Our Boy's Day

I didn't really appreciate a clean house until I had kids. Before they came around I kept things pretty well in order. The rotting vegetables in the fridge were rare and spotted early. The floors and surfaces were always clear, though I will admit, corners were, well, utilized I guess would be the right word.

After we had kids all that took a back seat. We are catching up and have a house you could walk into without causing us great embarrassment about 4 or 5 nights a week. We both work full time and don't have the spare cash to pay for people to clean. So when my wife asked if I'd like to take the guys out for a few hours this past Saturday so she could do a 'full clean' I jumped on the opportunity.

It was a super-hot and steamy morning and I lured them out to the car with a promise of driving to the playground. Now a playground offer has a 90% plus hit rate with my boys. They love a playground. But when it's a playground we have to drive to there is no stopping them as they hurtle out the door and hustle into their seats. Today was no exception. There was a brief moment of curious concern when I started the car and mommy wasn't in it.

'Where's mommy?' Teddy asked. 'She's staying home to clean. We're having a boy's day!'

We tend to travel as a pack on weekends. It's a cool stage of life, right now. For all its inefficiency the fact that we do everything together is cool. I'm still able to get some quiet time at night and we get as much cleaning done day to day as our energy will allow us after we've gotten them to sleep for the night. This boy's day was a departure from the norm. A notable one.

The park was fun and dangerous and exciting. Evidence of the differing nature of 'boy's day' came early.

'Daddy, I have to go to the bathroom.' Charlie said.

I scanned the perimeter. No bathrooms in sight. There was a tree line, though. Hm...

'Okay, buddy. We're going to the woods. Teddy!'

So off we trekked to learn a key skill of boyhood, how to effectively and respectively relieve oneself in nature. I would never have guessed this, but it felt fatherly to be in the woods with the boys, making sure they were out of sight from the other kids and parents. Making sure that they were off the trail sufficiently and coaching them on how to position themselves so they had the best cover. Also, walking back it felt like we were the cool kids. The rebels.

It really was the biggest of big playgrounds and there was plenty of fun and exploring to do. But the day had to move on and we had to run an errand. We were heading to the mall to get a replacement line for the weed-eater because there was supposedly a good deal at Sears. Not the type of thing we'd make a special trip for typically, but we were giving mom all the time she needed to clean and it was the mall with the indoor playground so it was enticing all on its own.

There is no greater place to entertain to little boys then in the section of Sears where we looked for and failed to find the weed-eater line replacement. It was heaven. They were climbing on and pretend driving the ride on mowers, hiding in and around the sheds for sale. Teddy actually stopped at the push mower, the kind with no motor, and gasped, 'So cool!' Mind you, he had no idea the utility of the thing. He just knew he wanted to play with it. It was actually harder to get them out of there than it was to get them off the playground.

Thankfully, the 'indoor playground' has taken up a spot in their imagination over the years that has magnified it's scale way out of proportion. I get it. I remember the excitement of coming across a McDonald's with a playground on vacations when I was young. It's so much fun to get caught up in these small extravagances with these guys. Excitement may be fleeting but it has yet to become something they control. When something, anything, hits them as exciting they burst and beam and giggle.

It's a great thing this indoor play station. A chance to sit and let them roam free. Increasingly the generation so many lament who spend all day looking at their phones and seeming disengaged are the ones having kids and this little respite in their day, a chance to scroll and to check in with the world they miss is as exciting for them (us!) is pretty exciting for them to.

Before too long we were off. Turned out that no one could assure us that there wasn't soy or sesame or peanuts or tree nuts in any of the mall food so our attempts to grab lunch failed. So we went where the 'food' was safe for my guys. While the disappointment of not being able to get a doughnut (soy) was real, it being replaced by a trip to the candy shop was more than enough to compensate. That's how we ended up with two bags of cotton candy. The little one doesn't even like cotton candy. No bother, he just wanted to have the chance to hold the same big bag his brother had.

So the day was over and we were headed back to our clean home and some fun times with mommy. The clouds had appeared and we weren't upset to spend the afternoon watching movies.

Boy's days won't last forever and they don't honestly come around enough. But the truth is that I can't get enough of them. Won't get enough of them. Ever.

Grabbing Life, Holding On

With every age and stage there come certain signs. Signs that my little boys are running out of time to be 'little boys'. It's not such a bad thing. In fact, for them it's the most exciting thing you could imagine. The walls are starting to come down. Well, perhaps not, but they are certainly moving further and further out and for my sweet rambunctious boys this is very, very exciting. From time to time they will pretend they are babies. Not in any real way, but they will say, 'I'm a baby...' in a silly voice, smile, giggle and laugh at the absurdity. They are decidedly little boys and we are accepting as best we can that we'll never have our babies again.

Like so many parents before us, we know they will always be our babies. It'll be a metaphor to them, but it won't be to us. They will be our two and only babies and we will hold them, if only in our hearts, as closely and tenderly as if they were newly wrapped and leaving the hospital for the first time for the rest of our lives.

But that will be it. The rest of our lives. The seemingly inexhaustible but ever diminishing time we have left with them, here amongst them, able to hug and be hugged is also being put into stark relief with each barrier breached and each new independence learned and granted. As they go through life reveling in the ever greater autonomy of being a 'big boy' another tiny tick passes and we are closer to the end. Not noticeably so, not always, but the big ones can pierce the bubble we've so happily stayed in during these early years. Can make us aware if not of our own ticking clocks then those of their time left in the bubble we've created and cared for and patched up and loved. As they grab life that is out there waiting for them we are hard pressed to let go of another tiny piece of it that we'd give anything to keep in our grasp until the end of time.

It's joyous. I don't want you to misunderstand. It's a faint feeling of time passing and is easily overwhelmed by the joys we share as they start there journey's. But it is a real feeling. A real sense of life's passing. We are older parents and we aren't so quick to let feelings slide passed as we once were. I suppose that's true for all parents, regardless of age. But with the years we bring to the task comes a thought that this second act that will happen when they no longer need the minute to minute, the meal to meal, the day to day or week to week attention they once did may be more on the down slope of our time here, our time with them. It's jarring to think, but comforting as well. As long as we can make it long enough to know they are safe, to know they are loved and to know that they know how wonderful this all is, than knowing this is the thing, being a parent and doing our best to make foster this family, we're pretty happy having that be the thing we go out on. The last and best of what we did while we were so lucky to be here.

I Hate School

I hate school. I hope you won't but I fear you will.

Let me be clear. I don't fear you will fail at school. You are INSANELY smart and I suspect you will soar at school. My fear is that school will fail you. That it will turn your attention from satisfying and stirring curiosity to simple and attainable achievement. That a fire you carry will dim in order that the oxygen it would have taken to be stoked from a flame to an inferno will be otherwise deployed to satisfy the wishes of others. It's hard to stay away from that. You'll spend lots of energy pursuing that which you may be unsure of to pursue the expectations you are handed. A little of that is okay, good even. But only enough to learn that you aren't here alone and you are accountable to others. Beyond that my only wish is that you find that which excites you and you pursue it without fear, embracing the failures that come from trying new things. Staying true to yourself will make most failures tolerable and some downright necessary. Just remember that failures are not end points. They are merely spots on the journey.

School made me horribly self-critical. I don't know why but it did. As you prepare to head out for your first day you are so much more prepared than I was. Still I find myself regressing. I sat with your mother last night and it all came out. I'm horrified and angry that you are heading to school. I had a miserable first few years at school and as a result I learned how to be liked regardless of whether or not I was remaining true to myself. I lacked confidence and swam in conformity. As much as I could. My heart and mind were free, but under wraps. All that time and energy spent hiding me made me wonder if I was worth anything.

If anyone ever laughs at you or says something critical about who you are ignore them. Seriously. Hold on to your kind heart, smart head, unique tastes and your loving and weird family. If you do you'll see these clowns for who they are. Okay, there was a tad more anger in this sentiment than intended. Truth is most of them are scared and excited and wanting to hide in a corner unnoticed while also wishing to have all the attention possible. Growing up is confusing sometimes. The only power anyone has over your opinion of yourself is the power you grant them. Don't give it. Hold firm. You are weird and wonderful and unique and perfectly flawed and loved. Find the people that are engaged in the things you want to be doing, regardless of what anyone else thinks about them, and sit with them. If it takes weeks or months or years, I don't care. Stay where you want to be, don't go where you're 'supposed' to be.

I love you so much and for one of the few times since meeting you I'm shaken. It caught me off guard. I've been spouting the 'I hate school' gospel for over 35 years now. But I didn't realize how much I feared it until I was seeing it through your eyes. Seeing it from a perspective of a protective dad, as someone who is certain that school worked in reverse, at least for me. It killed enthusiasm, stoked self-consciousness, raised fear and followed through on it. I know this won't happen to you, so why am I now thinking thoughts I haven't thought since I was your age. Feeling scared that kids might make fun of your stuff. Hoping to god you aren't picked on. Feeling a visceral concern that you have the wrong hair or wrong shirt or wrong glue sticks and you'll react like I did.

This is your journey and I have to check out of it. It's a hard pill to swallow, but this part of me, I have to protect you from it. Maybe when you are older we can talk about it. When we are two adults. Not now.

You really are going to do amazing things. You're going to LOVE school! YOU are going to make friends today that will be your friends for the next 13 years and probably for the rest of your life.

YOUR LIFE. I'm sorry if I forget that at times.

How To Put Your Kids To Bed In Whateverthef*ck Amount Of Steps

Hello! I'll be your child sleep guru. Leave your exhaustion and frustrations at the door because I'm here to help!

First a little about me... I'm a once proud man who has given himself over fully to parenthood. I'm a tad too heavy (actually it ranges from a tad to 'grossly', but that's just a medical term) and happier for learning how to cry and doing it 5-7 nights a week. But don't fret, these are tears of exhaustion and we all know there are different kinds of crying. I have very little sorrow these days and a great deal of joy (and exhaustion. Did I mention exhaustion?)

Like most parents we struggled with getting our children on a sleep schedule. There were tired, sleep deprived days and restless, exhausting nights. We struggled. But eventually we found ourselves in a routine of sorts. I don't really know how, but there were a few months, I think, a couple winters back, maybe, when we were done and the house was cleaned up (a relative status during these early years) by say, 9 o'clock. These were the glory days. But then we did what any smart parents would do and changed who put who to bed. I mean, I wanted some time with the little one and she was missing the big one, so we switched it up. Shouldn't be a big deal, but they disagreed. Both of them. So, there we were pulling our hair out. Trying over and over to get them to accept going to bed alone. Together. Apart. Whatever. Nope.

Then we figured it out. Here it is. The fail proof plan for getting your kids to sleep.

- **First things first. Have a healthy late afternoon snack.** I find this is a good time to reward positive behavior with sugar. It's not that I don't get the dangers, it's just they love it so much and surely they've sat still or played together or at the very least spent a portion of time not hitting anyone or throwing anything. That kind of self-control deserves a reward. Besides, bedtime is far enough off for them to really be able to burn off anything you might give them. Salty processed snacks work as well.

- **Ease into dinner with some screen time** Nothing big, but mine are 5 and 3. Perhaps they can do it on the deck. Get some fresh air.

- **Get the table ready for a good old fashioned family dinner** At least that way they will have a sense that there is another way, not plopped on couches in front of the TV. Occasionally me and the Mrs. even sit at the table al0ne and catch up. It's nice. Plus nothing goes with nuggets quite like Octonauts and Lego Batman programs.

- **After dinner let's all go to our separate corners** After you've devolved into trading M&M's for bites of string beans there's a natural tension that needs to be released. We tend to hide in the kitchen gorging on the M&M's they didn't earn while they go slightly bananas in the living room and backyard.

- **Now that we've all calmed down let's bribe them into a bath** This works about 50% of the time. Frankly they've developed enough methods to get all the rewards they could want and by now they usually are tired of candy.

- **Sure. It's 8:30. Let's get one more show in.**

- **Okay. I blew that one. I should have been putting on PJ's and brushing teeth... But on the bright side I'm all caught up on Facebook. One more show. A quiet one.**

- **Okay, NOW I'm all caught up on Facebook. Final show, Sarah and Duck, it's the right thing for bedtime.** I will skip over the professional wrestling moves often incorporated in subduing a 3 year old to brush his teeth. He's stronger than you can imagine.

- **Hit the sheets.** And of course by that I mean we bunker down, literally lying in bed with them. Some will say this is not the right way. Many actually. That's all.

- **Bathroom. Can't say no and we don't want them wetting the bed** Also, we have one who has made it his strategy to power down as many liquids as possible at about eight. It's just good policy to let him go when he asks.

- **Lie in bed with them as they wear themselves out with a thousand stuffed animals that they only play with in bed.** As I read this I'm starting to wonder why we even keep them. At the very least we shouldn't keep them in their room. I'm pretty sure I have this thought every night.

- **Snap. Yell. Bark at your three year old that you've had enough. GO TO SLEEP.** The predictable tears are the worst because it was your own lack of self-control that brought them. Now you are both emotional wrecks. Kids recover quicker. This becomes the guilt and shame that weighs your shoulders down and gives you cravings for ice cream

- **Apologize. Make boundaries. One big stuffed dog and one more animal. And that's it.**

- **Buckle under and allow them all the stuffed animals they want.**

- **Cry in the dark.** As long as you control your own breathing they shouldn't notice.

- **Fall asleep while they play in the bed.** Let's face it, you're exhausted anyway.

- **Finally, now that you are unconscious and non-responsive, somehow, they fall asleep.**

- **Wake up, eyes puffy from crying yourself to sleep.**

- **Look over and see your sleeping three year old.** My goodness. He's an angel.

- **Take pride in his development.** Technically he fell asleep on his own!

- **Go back downstairs and cry the tearless sobs of a parent starting to clean a disaster area just before midnight.** Cleaning, though annoying, will ease just enough tension to allow you to relax into a slouch on the couch in a half cleaned living room with a thing of Ben & Jerry's or some Pringles.

- **Wash it all down with a giant plastic tumbler of boxed wine.**

The best designs are simple, elegant. Give up. Give in. Eat Ice Cream. Drink wine.

The best we do so much of the time is to keep them alive and get out of the way. I'm good at the first part, still working on getting out of the way..

Picture Day

Today is picture day. You are wearing a new blue button down shirt and we packed a more durable, comfortable shirt in your bag for you to wear at after school. I have my suspicions as to whether you'll change, though. You are so proud of yourself today and you know you are handsome. It doesn't occur to you to be bashful, to quell your pride. You smiled this morning and you were excited. Today is picture day.

Picture day is a day for us too. It's a day to get a snapshot of you in Kindergarten. A chance for us to attempt earnestly to do the impossible. To capture you as you are now, to freeze you in this moment. We do it so we can share this moment with the wide world of people that love you. To capture and disseminate your joyful boyishness so that even a tiny bit can be transported across space and your Grandma and Koba and Nana and Papa can hold this part of you from hundreds of miles away. So they can put you on the fridge and look at you whenever they wish. So they can show their friends and your relatives, ones you don't even know yet, how well you are doing. So they can feel pride. Not only in you, but in us.

We also take these pictures so that we, your mommy and daddy, can travel through time to right now. It's important. We dress you in your finest and we do your hair especially carefully. I think you may have even had your first encounter with hairspray this morning. We do it as it is our wont. We want you to look your finest and be happy. So we can find this picture a few years from now when you are perhaps a bit self-conscious and less open to us combing your hair. When you try to comply and smile, but when that smile is put on, something to think about and not so much your default facial expression. We will come back in time to this picture and the others like it to remember who you are inside, at least the part of who you are that we first met. We'll always see that part, even after you're convinced it's not there anymore. We'll know it's just dormant. You will never look like you do now and that's important to memorialize, but you will feel this way again, but it will be tempered by life and what it teaches you.

Innocence is highly overrated. But it is also a real and wonderful part of being five and while you are a more mature boy every day and while we love that you can be quiet and contemplative from time to time, there is something we will miss about this time you are rapidly graduating from where you are earnest and honest with us and yourself by default. You haven't gotten too caught up in fitting in. Too caught up in trying on identities you conjure. Instead you look at the camera proud because you are handsome, funny, smart and loved and you know it. And so do we.

We'll know it when you are away at college and going on adventures to find yourself. When you are busy developing and defining your purpose. We will look at this picture and the others, the ones from every step on the way and we will be recognizing ours. We will see all that went in to getting you to picture day and take pride in us, all of us, for doing what we did together. We will still be doing it, but it will look a lot different than it does now, all of us smooshed together, experiencing it as one and interpreting it individually. There might be times when these interpretations are deceptive and we struggle to stay positive. You may need to distance yourself and we may reactively hold tighter. You'll surely have to push us away someday, just like we will surely have to nudge you along from time to time. It will all be from love, but it might not always feel that way. When it doesn't these pictures will help.

They'll help you too. You'll look back and remember vividly some things. I remember my mother wetting the comb and working with my cowlick. Trying over and over to suppress my hairs natural desires in an attempt to look my best. Licking her thumb and cleaning the smudges from my cheek. I remember the brown bags we used for lunches that my father would sit at the table at night and decorate. I'll remember the joyful pink elephant sitting under the lone palm tree on the tiny island on a lunch bag that I used repeatedly that I loved so much that he made for me. It's another framed talisman from a time gone by that I cling to, though after my many adult moves I can't say I know exactly where it is. I'll find it someday, probably too late, and when I do I'll cry tears of love and joy.

Hopefully when you look back, from a great distance and see your picture you'll see love. The love and time and unabashed joy we took in giving you what we had. In doing our best to make sure you were taken care of, that you knew you were loved. Because when we look at them, when we travel through time and space to see the you you are now it will be with joy. It will be with love. It will be with longing for the time we had with you and the many journeys' you are surely going to take.

I Am Dad

It was a massive transformation and now I'm *transformed.*

Parenthood is a sequence of workaday realities that once awed and floored me in a way that when not paralyzing, was heartbreakingly beautiful and expansive. Well, it's still those things, really, I just can't throw as much emotional energy behind it all anymore. I am still transported on a daily basis to a place of awe and wonder, but it's often fleeting. It has to be. Any moment of daydreaming and self-reflection is necessarily interrupted by the mundanity of daily life with a 5 and freshly minted 4 year old.

Gone is the exhaustion fueled deluge of emotional frailty and excruciatingly earnest expressions of fawning and perspectiveless love. It is not as sad as it sounds. These feelings are still there, behind all the work. Gone however is the constant feeling of being overmatched by the task at hand. It's been replaced by a security you only have when you have a steady hand and a clear eyed confidence that you are up to the task.

Sure, we could feed them better food, we could replace TV shows and movies with family activities, we could certainly stand to reduce screen time and increase story time. We could even take better care of ourselves come to think of it. We could sleep more. We could drink more water and less wine (okay, I'm the wine drinker). We could be more physical and less sedentary. We could stand to spend less time on our screens and could be more patient and less prone to yelling. Where was I going with this... ?

Whatever. All of it is to say we got this. We get a ton wrong, but we're doing it. Not everything is a trauma and drama. We've left the bubble where reflection and exploration were how we retained a sense of self as we changed to who we needed to become.

Being a parent, a dad, is now a fully ingrained part of me. It's who I am and I'm no longer struggling to fit into this new uniform. It's on and worn in at this point. My mistakes are not as often the learning and growing experiences they once were. Now they are just human. Just what it's like being this guy.

What hasn't changed is the love. The fascination. The endless desire to be connected to these people. My tiny tribe. Karen and I have rediscovered each other and it's never been better. We've never been closer or more in love. The kids are still orbiting us, tied to our motions and our decisions and our schedule but they are drifting. They have interests beyond us and it's amazing to us what is so natural to anyone else. It amazes us simply because we have all of the wonder and awe of the first time they opened there eyes stored in our hearts and to see them venture and wander, well, it can make you swallow hard and hold back a tear now and again. Just as fast the moment passes and we are swept up into the day to day grind of running a house, a car service, a grocery and a restaurant (specializing in nuggeted nutrition of dubious value), a recreation department, an education system, social services organization, a health and safety inspection unit, a counseling service and cleaning service (which is a failing venture if ever there was one) and to a degree we never could have before, we love doing it. It's our life's work. For now the emphasis is on work but down the road, and not too far, it'll be understood much more so as our life.

Fragile and Brave

I have a picture of you from daycare. You are sitting quietly, legs stretched out in front of you. You are holding a board book, eyes down inspecting it. Your cheeks are so beautiful I can feel them just by looking, smooth, soft and pink with warmth. Your narrow shoulders are somewhere under the hood of your sweatshirt, a book open but ignored between your legs as you investigate this other book that has captured your curiosity. You're wearing jeans and there are books scattered around you. You're probably an old 2 year old in this picture, or maybe a young 3 year old. You are fully engaged, busy doing and uninterested in the person standing in front of you, probably unaware of their presence, who took the shot. I love this picture and it can make me cry.

You are the youngest and I can't stop seeing the vulnerable in you. Sitting here with the picture and without you I can't for the life of me imagine you look any different than that picture. Cherubic and intrigued. Tiny and determined. But you have grown. A lot. I still see the baby in you and always will.

You still tell me about 'tomachakes' (stomach aches) and love 'Sharlie' (Charlie) and I don't really want you to learn you are mispronouncing these things. I don't want you to grow up.

There are selfish reasons that mostly live in my subconscious. For one, if you're getting older than I'm getting older. You don't need to really know this for a good long time now, but I'm not going to be here forever and when I see you lost in discovering I want to freeze the world and stay in it forever. I didn't have heaven until I met you and Charlie. Mommy made me come to life in a way I hadn't, but the concept of heaven was one I rejected for lack of imagination. To be fair, who could conceive of something so wonderful and extraordinary as you. My heaven is here and now.

Another reason I prefer you stay in this moment forever is so that I can always be what I am to you right now and you can always be what you are to me. We have challenging moments for sure, but they are fleeting. They revolve around simple challenges. This simplicity is balanced by an extraordinary frequency. You can have 5-8 crises before breakfast and without fail, whether we do so well or poorly, we get through every one.

Thirdly, I fall asleep next to you. You don't like to fall asleep. You love to sleep, but the falling part, you are a resister. You get this from me. Each night, when I see you are tired, when we've been lying in bed for a long time I'll inevitably say, 'just close your eyes, buddy.' Without fail, at least to this point in time it's always met with your response of, 'But it hurts to close my eyes.' I could stop asking, but I just love the answer so much. You'll start to drift and most nights you'll pop your head up and say one last, half conscious crazy non-sequitur just before rolling over and falling asleep. Something like 'I can't sleep in parking lot frogs' or 'I look just like Fawzy.' In case you're wondering years from now what those things mean, well, I have no idea on the frog thing, but the 'Fawzy' thing is how you pronounce 'Quazi'. He's a character from Octonauts and your mispronunciation is adorable. I prompt it like five times a day.

What I really don't want to change is the you in this picture. You are a perfectly fine with the contradictory nature of life that becomes something so scary as an adult. You are exquisitely fragile and profoundly brave at the same time all the time. It's amazing to see. Your brother was the same way, but you learn, you will learn any day now, to be self-conscious. You will wonder how other people will react before pursuing an interest. You will stop crying when mad and sometimes even try not to laugh when something is funny. You'll toughen up and as a result you'll be more cautious. That's the confounding conundrum you're going to wrestle with in the years ahead. It's okay, you're supposed to. But what is going on right here and now is beautiful and not be dismissed hastily.

Being simultaneously fragile and brave has served you extremely well to now. It's made you explore nature intuitively and voraciously. Left to your own free will you'd spend hours a day trying to find and transport every imaginable living creature from the dirt back to the house to show us. You explore whatever sparks your curiosity and you do it with abandon. You are excited when you see things you love, so excited you barely keep in your skin and you show it with squeals. They are pure joy and they are infectious to all who hear them. When you are upset, regardless of any reason or the presence of any others you let that be known too. Your emotions come out when they are felt and it's incredibly healthy. In a sense you taught me these things. Charlie did too, but he's teaching us other things. He's at the tip of the spear, bringing us to new experiences all the time. He's a boundary breaker and we can't really enjoy as much of that process as we can with you. He's desensitized us and you are showing us how to live an experience, not just survive it.

I can honestly say that you've impacted my life more than I ever could yours. You've shown me the value of being unafraid. You've pushed me to challenge my fears to explore my world like you do yours. Thank you.

I feel extraordinarily fragile these days. I also feel brave and curious. All these things were pushed so far down before I knew you that I often felt nothing, which was perfect for keeping invisible, but terrible for feeling alive. Living is pursuing your curiosity and finding your emotions and wrestling with all of it all the time. Living is not fearing feelings, but feeling them, saying it and processing them fully and with the help of those you love so you can put them down and not be ruled by them. Living is something you can only do if you are fragile and brave, just like you.

Funny Boys

Charlie: *I like this one.*

Teddy: *I like pick pun*

Charlie: *What's a 'pick pun'?*

Teddy: *Um.. It's a kind of pun?*

Charlie: *What's a 'pun'?*

Teddy: *It's a type of berry.*

****

These conversations happen all the time now. So often I don't even hear them. They are part of the white noise of parenthood, the ever present hum that fills the background of our lives and colors the corners of the spaces we share. They are amazing and we hardly ever notice them. But we were in the car and I happened to note the entire exchange. Once it hit me I couldn't stop laughing. Like, fully exhaled, tears coming, hysterical laughter. This was brilliantly funny.

First is the simple mock of 'I like pick pun.' This is a four year old's greatest tool when confronting an irresistible force such as an older brother with whom he is endlessly enamored with and to whom he feels the yoke of tyranny. The force is strong in Teddy and he will be free the yoke sooner than I might even imagine, but for now the older brother is living up to his first born obligations as an authoritarian leader. He can't and won't be dissuaded, though we do check his power whenever we see him abusing it. We're even preemptive if we think any situation, from which order to eat his dinner to how long he is entitled to play with his own toys before 'sharing' them (like a feudal tax) to his (tor)mentor, the older brother.

Charlie, for his part, ever the straight man in this entire exchange, took his younger brother at face value. He was genuinely curious as to what a 'pick pun' was. The air of my second child changed. What was a playful, mocking tone immediately became something far more worthy of genuine consideration. His idol and hero noticed him. He asked him a question. He was interested in what was being said to him! I could practically hear his inner monologue as he pondered what to say now that he'd found himself here. 'OMG, this is really happening. He wants to know something that I can tell him... Don't blow it... What is a pick pun, what is a pick pun.. 'It's a kind of pun..' '

A good deal of the humor was in this shift from total silliness to serious.

'What's a pun' said Charlie.

It worked! Teddy tested the waters with nonsensical logic and he bought it. He was on the line. This was more than a bite.. Now, how to reel him in..

'It's a type of berry.'

Talk about nailing the dismount...Brilliant! My boy is a creative genius!

Some might say that this simple exchange is not worthy of this level of line by line analysis. To them I say leave the assessment of my child's genius to me. For now I will proceed knowing that regardless of whether or not these boys decide to develop this act, regardless of whether they choose the fame and riches of comedy genius, it doesn't matter. Perhaps they will find more fulfillment in some other line of endeavor. But I'll know, I'll always know that they will always have this talent to fall back on. Not only as a career, but as a tool to navigate everything from meeting people to handling rejection. These boys are legit and the 'yes and' crowd should keep an eye on this up and coming improvisational duo.

What's a pick pun.

It's a kind of pun.

Genius!

Let's Talk About Sex (Now That You Have Kids)

We've been DTF since jump. It's one of those things I guess. Pretty happy to find that it's hardly diminished in quality despite the rapid aging and overall physical toll raising kids has had on me. No, quality is not the issue. Our problem is quantity.

That's right. This is a married, middle aged sex post. There's nothing graphic to scare you away, though the topic is the topic. Grab a glass of wine or a cold one and see if any of what I'm saying strikes a chord. If you know me and have no wish to think of me as a sexual being and it's already too late as I referenced my sexual life already and you have inadvertently and regretfully already constructed a horrifying picture in your mind I'd advise you go find the old bottle with the handle in the liquor cubby. The one in the back you bought for a super bowl party 15 years back and just guzzle. After slamming your computer shut or throwing your phone away and smashing it like those guys with the fax machine in Office Space, erase all record of me. Wake up, check that you retained enough senses to unfollow, unfriend and unremember me before blacking out and move on with your life. Nothing to see here.

I don't want to hear any morality nonsense. Firstly we're married so discussing the beautiful coming together (Not literally. Too high risk. We are committed turn takers, a stance I'll defend to the death.) of a portly man who retains mere glimmers of his former beauty and his ageless, perfect wife (Seriously. Think Peter and Lois of the Griffin family. This image will reflect the vast disparity between her physical appeal and mine. It's great to be in it, for me at least. Can't speak for the wife, but I don't need any photos either so I get where you might be coming from. Pics of her, yes, yes, a thousand times yes, but yeah, as for me, nah.. That's a hard pass (Boom)) is decidedly in bounds. As far as your pearl clutching at the idea of middle aged folks doing the deed, I just don't care anymore. Don't let anyone tell you there are NO advantages to becoming an old man and losing your fastball. I may be a junk baller now (boom) but at least I no longer care about your opinions regarding my life. It's remarkably freeing getting old.

So, anyway...

Here's my complaint. We would love to have more 'alone time' then we get. Let's not beat around the bush (boom), it's all their fault. These little, well, let's just say 'rhymes with dockblockers' are unwitting masters of their chosen form. It ain't just the simple stuff either. There's plenty of that garden variety salt in their game, sure. There's more though. They're playing the long game as well. Let me show you what I mean.

Sex is a generous and warm way for us to give and receive love. It's great for that. Do you know when those feelings of love are often stirred? When you are being that version of your family that you hoped you'd be as you strolled out of that hospital, baby in hand wondering, 'Holy crap. Is no one going to stop me? Am I just allowed to take this person home? What the hell. I don't think I'm tall enough for this type of responsibility.' Say after grabbing pumpkins and cider at the farm market. Everyone was cute in their autumnal sweaters and cords. Maybe I threw on those jeans that make me feel sexy. A flirty scarf might have even been thrown on last minute. Why not? We're worth it. For a sunny, crisp afternoon it was easy to think we were the couple we impersonate in our professionally staged family photos. It felt great!

So great that we lost our heads. We started making out in the kitchen while lunch was being defrosted in the toaster oven and the kids were distracted by the Curious George Halloween special on Netflix. These were heady times. We should have proceeded with caution. But we didn't. That's kinda the point of heady times.

'Wanna have some sexy time..' one of you says.

'Hell yeah! I'm a man ain't I?' one of us replies. Okay. It was me. 'I mean seriously. I am right? I can still do this right?' My lady is my support in many ways and confidence is a fleeting thing in your forties. At least in so far as physical prowess goes. At least for me it is. Stop judging me. Move on.

'After the kids go to bed.'

Ohmygodohmygodohmygod... That's it. That's the time we can do it (boom)! She's serious.

'Yes. Oh my god, yes!' I reply.

'I don't know, they're looking pretty beat at the moment.' It's a joke, but you know, whatevs. She's digging me.

This is a good day. There's a ton left to do and seemingly endless hours until we reach the Promised Land. But it shines in my minds like a beacon on a hill as I climb. Through meals, laundry, cleaning, laundry, playing, cleaning, laundry and folding laundry and bath time all the way until we put them to bed. Through it all we stole kisses and wayward grabs, having fun and laughing. Smiling and flirting, knowing we knew what was coming (boom) and we were excited for it. Fueled by lust and love and coffee we finally arrived at nightfall. Kids fed, cleaned, watered and pottied there was only one hurdle left to clear.

This is where our 'bad' parenting comes in. Please note, we are wonderful parents. They are nearly as lucky to have us as we are to have them. But the component skills of parenthood, the things one must master to be able to sustain without losing your mind daily, well, we haven't been great about those things. This is never more evident than at bedtime.

To be fair the look we have by now, sun having gone down (we never really adhered to that early to bed approach so many successful put-to-bedders have ascribed) baths and meals prepared and given, our energy is waning. But that's okay. Our enthusiasm for the endeavor remains. We give one another a wink as we head to separate bedrooms and begin the long day's journey into slumber. Falling asleep is not a default reaction to being tired. So the nightly wrestling match begins. I can't speak for her but in our room, it's almost impossible to survive the process with anything approaching an iota of energy left.

Thus begins the 'dockblocking' of which I noted.

Board books. Curse thee. Sure, some are better than others. I get that.. I can get down with the Little Blue Truck. I have a love hate relationship with Goodnight Moon. I can certainly appreciate the cleverness of the assorted Seussian delights that dot the bookshelf (piles next to the bed) of my kid's bedroom. The problem is that they are a very VERY powerful narcotic once you've read them, in the right order, 200 times or so. By now, 1800+ readings in, it's positively deadening. The ability to read an entire book with my eyes closed, turning the page at the right times is a cool trick, sure. But it's accompanied so often by my kid, bright eyed and bushy tailed turning to wake me up and force more of this on me. Any more of this little blue truck and a little blue pill wouldn't even be able to get me to the 'finish line' of our earlier promise.

Next, lights out and in bed. More 'bad at parenting' here. We have never had the will to let them shed a tear in pursuit of sleep. We've tried but our inevitable, lily livered buckling has left these boys unable to close their eyes without us lying next to them. For, at times, hours. This is the death of me. More often than not when my forty something constitution collides with their toddler level energy for a whole day I am unaware, perhaps, but the game is over. Long over by this point. Let's say, by some miracle I don't fall asleep with my kids. Just for arguments sake. This series of events, this hustle (I'm convinced they are doing this on purpose to keep me away from mommy) has already worked.

As I exit the room I am weary. My ears are hot with exhaustion and I'm long overdue for bed. Having taken the hours I was expected to take my wife, having succumbed as well, in her own way to the other one in the other room has decided that I'm not coming out. On goes the jammys and the robe. These are not anything other than comfortable and delightful. I too am in my formless, baggy, old and tattered 'sleep shorts'. We are not ideally clothed for this endeavor, but it could happen. We are kid free. At least we should be for the next 3-5 hours when kid 2 makes his way to our bed. We let him sleep there. It's in line with our other poor decisions, it really shouldn't surprise you. By the time we are on the couch, either said or not, that's it. Ballgame (sad boom) over.

I should note there is germ warfare at play as well. In general we all have varying degrees of chest and head colds at all times. This wasn't true before they showed up. I'm not accusing them of purposeful espionage, per se. I'm not ruling it out though. For whatever the reasons might be symptoms get real persistent at these times. I doubt this is intentional, but again, I don't rule it out.

That's it. More often than not this is how sexy time plays (itself) out in our house. Stoked by feelings of warm connectedness. Given oxygen with stolen kisses and hidden grabs. Promised and anticipated. Doused. Dissipated.

Our Adventures..

I'm running out of nights like this. I lie in the dark trying to get comfortable in a single bed with a big four year old that wants me there and wants me out of his way all at once. We talk a lot about how he doesn't want to sleep, how he doesn't know how to sleep. We used to talk about how closing his eyes hurt him. I've since learned to stop asking him to close those eyes.

This is all after I've read the 6 year old as much Harry Potter (we're on 'Chamber of Secrets' and he seems to love it!!) as I can before my eyes fail or his drift off. I love that we've gotten to the Harry Potter stage, even if I did rush it a little. The natural magnetic force keeping us ever connected is loosening as he ventures out in the world and our relationship is evolving, as it should. I'm happy we're taking these nightly adventures to Hogwarts. I loved reading these books the first time around, but for me that was my 20's and 30's. Reading with him is making me acutely aware and evermore enchanted by all I am seeing now that I'm experiencing it all with a little guy who is more able to see the wonder and magic that Harry Potter and his friends and their escapades have to offer.

I haven't always relished the putting the kids to sleep thing. Until recently we were each taking one kid and not getting out until real late, at which time we'd start the nightly cleanup. I'd be grumpy and tired and frustrated and my wife, far better at transitioning than I, would be left looking for adult conversation with a brooding lump who couldn't be bothered to take his headphones all the way off. If you ask my wife I could still probably use an exit room akin to those ones I've seen in therapist's offices on sitcoms. A place to process my feelings and decompress after putting the boys to bed.

Making the transition to the daddy that shares an interest with a kid from one who is the caretaker is one that happens organically. You recognize it piece by piece. You mark it in books first. Lifted his head, rolled over, first solid food, crawled, first words, first steps. Somehow they feel like your own accomplishments. To a small degree they are and in perspective they are amongst the most important minor roles you'll ever take in any endeavor in your life. But they aren't yours. These things, all of them, are there's. We get the early credit as we should, but they are emerging. Each milestone marking a tick further along as they make it all the way to the people they will be. We are so caught up documenting every tree that the forest grows up around us and behind us and without us noticing we are wrapped up in discovering the life we missed along the way. Understanding the journey we made from lifting our heads and rolling over all the way to now. In doing so we learn that we were magical creatures once too. We were once the tour guides of life for the great adventurers we were once so unable to notice as they were disguised as our parents.

Eventually it's an adventure inside an adventure inside an adventure out into infinity. We can look backwards and imagine our lineage as a seemingly never ending line, emerging and submerging each to the next all the way to the horizon. I find myself endlessly curious about the lives of all of them. I lie in bed wondering if my own parents felt this strange mix of weary burden and enlightened awe as they lie in the dark wondering if they were doing it right. Did they ever lie in that bed as the defiant and playful 3 year old while their parents wondered why they were given so much to carry and so much to be carried by. It's all so obvious now, to me, this joy that I feel in the midst of the frustrations and among fluctuating confidence that can bounce so wildly between feeling absolutely assured that I'm nailing this whole parenting thing and the utter and obvious understanding that I am completely unequal to the task and am failing in ways that will inevitably go echoing into a future that scares me because I can't know how it will all turn out. If it will all turn out.

Before long I'm back to the story. Back to the excitement of seeing what will happen to the boy who lived under the stairs. Excited to see how he will once again foil the indefatigably awful Dursley's so he can make his way back to where he needs to be, with his friends, finding the life that is awaiting him. Full of adventure and meaning and life and love and tragedy. Hoping that he makes it through without the scars burdening him so greatly that he can't be who he was supposed to be. Hoping beyond hope that there's a story about the evil ones that makes it all make sense in a way that wasn't just pure evil. Hoping the Dursley's find peace and Harry can find forgiveness and understanding when he eventually gets to an age and thinks, 'What the hell was all that about?!' Hoping love will find each and every one of the people that matter. Hoping it will reach the Harry's and Ron's and Hermione's, sure, but also the Neville's and even the Draco's and Crabbe and Goyle's.

The adventure goes on far further than I ever imagined as a kid. It stretches out before me and beyond me ever morphing and suddenly surprising. The further I go the more I want. I lay in the dark adrift in adventure, wondering and wanting more than I ever could have thought imaginable while also knowing I won't be around to see it all play out.

My Sister

The family she arrived to

My earliest memory of my sister was of a man coming to our house to speak with my parents. He was there to see if our home was a stable one. One where my sister would be welcomed and provided for. One where she would not only be safe, but hopefully nurtured and loved. I remember my mom essentially asking me to be on my best behavior before they arrived, but who's to say whether or not that actually happened. I was, after all, just 6 years old.

I didn't really understand why we were getting another sister. I had 2 already. There were 3 of us boys. I don't think much of an effort was made to explain it, but that said, I have a six year old now and it's remarkable the things he doesn't hear us saying and the things he does. Maybe there was a giant family meeting. Maybe it was just the few words of encouragement to act normal when the interviewer came over to meet us.

Maya Lin (this is the name of the designer of the Vietnam Memorial and I will be using it in place of my sister's name in this post) was a teenage girl from Vietnam and we were a very big and ever growing family of white, suburban,

Great Lakes style Americans. We must have been quite a shock to her. Tall, pale and rambunctiously carefree. We were loud and curious, bold and kind. We were a station wagon with wood paneling kind of family who couldn't have been more American. I can't for the life of me, now, imagine what it was like for her to be dropped into this story as a young girl. At the time it never occurred to me to wonder.

I was not all that welcoming. It's just not a strength of little boys. I argued with her over the TV. A lot. To my memory my mom always sided with Maya. I was always cordial in screaming about how unfair it was and storming out of the room. I was a real charmer back then. Before long she acclimated. Never has more been swept aside in so short a time as me brushing past the acclimation process. But what can I know. She was plopped down into a new home and made a member of a new family in an instant. It was never questioned, never fretted on. Not from our side, my side at least.

Sure, my mother will tell you, if you ask, about that time, about her incredulous reaction to seeing snow fall, a thing she'd come accustomed to in no time as we lived in the 3rd snowiest city in America according to the video I watched on Facebook yesterday. It was from The Weather Channel and it meshes with my memory and the common understanding of where I'm from. She'll tell you about how she had to have the TV to watch Soap Operas, a thing that was banned in my house for the wild disregard for moral behavior, to learn the language. My mom, and I don't know how she figured this out, showed her these shows because all the characters spoke slowly, they over emoted, they spoke directly to the camera in close up and they repeated themselves over and over. Minus the horrid personal behavior, they were ideal for teaching the language. The other favorite was West Side Story. Musical theater courses through both sides of my family and while the appeal of this was lost on six year old me, the effect for language acquisition was also helpful. And she flat loved West Side Story. Mom would also tell you of her struggles acclimating to school and the challenge it was for her in that short time before she got the language down and made a friend or two.

I'd tell you about the new smells that as a 6 year old I thought were horrifying. This shouldn't shock anyone who's ever had a little boy. I had to leave the room the other day because I was eating a banana and this was just too much for Teddy to handle. In my case it was the smells of the food that I now realize I really missed out on. My palate has grown in sophistication since then and at this time when half my calories comes from cough drops and the other half comes from cold, discarded, nuggeted meats it feels like a real missed opportunity. Then there was the smell of bad over boiled hot dogs coming from the bathroom when her friend came over. It was just a home perm, a thing a thousand teenage girls that year did in my town, but none lived with us. My older brothers were yet to pull the trigger on the home perm.

Whatever her experience I can't tell you. But I can tell you that it was a fully family version of growing up. It was sadly not the ideal version of family that was taken from her. But it was a very loving one she made her way to and became a part of. And because she did I learned of the small but thriving Vietnamese community where we went to shop with her. I saw the food from all over the world I had never imagined existed so close to me. I learned the look of government issued, self-enveloping, light blue international letter paper that allowed her to get what I think were censored letters from her family in Vietnam. It taught me that I could love her in all the same complicated ways we all love our individual family members. I remember being sad when we dropped her off at college and happy when she could and would come home for holidays. I remember missing her way of eating; a thing you don't think can be different, so different before you see it. I remember feeling like something was missing when she wasn't there and feeling like we were all home when she was.

Our whole family was growing as this all took place. We were adding new members and each of us growing as well. By the time she was done with college she had a boyfriend. A Vietnamese boyfriend. I was 16(ish) and we were now 6 Medler's (My youngest brother was born in 84) and everyone that would be a part of our family had arrived, to one degree or another, by this point. Whether it was right after college or a few years later her boyfriend eventually asked her to marry him. She said yes.

The wedding was to be in King of Prussia, just outside of Philadelphia. I don't know why, but I think they were living there at the time. She worked at a bank, I know that much, but honestly, she could have been president or a part time teller. Regardless I now look back on her asking me to be in her wedding with immense pride. It's a real honor that she thought of me. I'm afraid at the time I was not so gracious. I said no. Yeah. I was also from a family where they respected my right to do such a thing. I'm sorry I did that. I'm incredibly thankful that they also asked my older brothers, both of whom have been and remain far more gracious in such matters.

Well, shortly before the wedding, and I mean very shortly, one of those government issued, self-enveloping, light blue international letters arrived to alert Maya that her whole family was being released (had been granted visa's.) I can't begin to imagine how this felt for her. She hadn't seen her mother and father and sisters and brothers since leaving. They hadn't seen her since she was taken away. I can't get into details I don't know, but I know that what happened in the time between her leaving home and arriving to us was scary. She was made to leave in a moment's notice and she was in a camp for some period of time. There were long periods when she was cargo on boats with no place to go, having no idea what life would hold if there was a future. She experienced and endured, as a teenage girl, innocent and surely terrified, things I know I never would have endured. But now she was here. My big sister. Annoying and loving. My honest to god sister. All the while waiting and hoping she could see her family again.

They would be arriving in a short time and once there the wedding would be in a matter of days. I remember us all, now in a minivan, making our way from Brockport New York down to Philly and checking into as few rooms as were reasonable for our large family, and getting dressed in our fancy duds. Mike and Eric in their tuxes and I in my Don Johnson whites (it was the 80's) and my sisters in their best. My parents were old pros. They left enough time for us to woof down some happy meals and such in the parking lot of the McDonalds before heading over to the wedding, where all the food would be stuff our sensibilities hadn't yet caught up to. I'm sure they were traditional Vietnamese wedding foods, but we weren't really the traditional Vietnamese wedding goers. Not by a long shot. My Abraham Lincoln looking father matched old Abe in every detail, even height and frame. 6'4" and slender, of Irish and Finnish descent. Still, we were there, her family. We weren't in the front row, as that was for her Vietnamese family, but we were ushers and participants, those of us wise enough to recognize and accept that honor. Again, very sorry.

Anyway, there I sat a foreigner in my homeland at a joyous celebration for my sister and her new husband. The ceremony was in Vietnamese and we knew to follow along. Our little League of Nations pew at the church each weekend was one that taught us how to be attuned to ritual and ceremony and this was no different. Just a different language. I remember looking back as the music started. My father and sister emerged, arm in arm. They walked down the aisle, she a bride and he her dad. It was beautiful. When they got to the first pew my father stopped, removed his arm and kissed her cheek and handed her hand to her father's arm who took her the rest of the way and ceremonially gave her away.

I can't imagine what this was like for her Vietnamese family. I can say that a lot of what I now see as extraordinarily meaningful was not so profound in the moment. I didn't realize it all, what it all meant at the time. I'm discovering layers even as I write it here.

Our lives take on different meanings as they beat ever forward. Contexts and understandings change as we do. I know that my sister was meant to be a part of my family. It may not have been predestined, it may have come as the result of wretched circumstance. But in the end the love that we had, that persists to this day as we are all flung far and wide is something I'm so thankful for.

'I Like That I'm Weird'

'Tell me something you love about yourself. What is something about you that you really like.' his mommy asked.

'I like that I'm weird. I like 'small potatoes'. I know it's supposed to be for little kids, but I like it anyways. I like that I'm weird like that.' Charlie said.

When Karen came down from putting him to bed she could barely contain how excited she was to tell me about this little conversation. She was right to be excited. I couldn't have been happier to hear it.

'I like that I'm weird.' How great is that?

Getting comfortable with my weirdness is something that's taken me a lifetime. First step for me was seeing that I was weird and trying with all my might to deny/hide it. Since then, since getting to a place where I passed as a normal I've been working like nobody's business to try to unburden myself of my various insecurities and collected disguises. I needed to conform, emotionally. I needed to fit in first. It left me safe and sad. Once there I needed to get back out, which was harder. It was definitely harder to reclaim my 'weird' than it was to fit in.

So to hear this news, well, I just wanted to wake him up and tell him how proud I was of him. I wanted to tell him he'd discovered the secret to happiness. I wanted to tell him that loving things you aren't 'supposed to' is something it took me forever to learn to do and longer to be comfortable saying I loved those things. I was so impressed with him. I wanted to open YouTube and start playing endless episodes of 'Small Potatoes' with him.

Furthermore I wanted to tell him that his life would forever be better as long as he is true to himself. If you like sports and that's not weird, so what, it's true. I guess that's it. I felt shame around my weirdness. Still do from time to time. Then I come here, I tell on myself and I learn to get comfortable being me. My weird self. My journey is as much about meeting me as it is about meeting the world and he has a moment now, one he can call back on and know, being weird, feeling different, it can be a huge gift!

I love my little weirdos so damn much.

The 7 Parents You Meet at Kids Birthday Parties

The boom of the 'Birthday-Industrial Complex' is among the most under reported developments in child rearing in the decades since I was reared. The strip malls that seemed to pop up out of fields and abandoned lots when we were coming into our own can no longer sustain the retail markets that augured their construction. So, there it was. Open spaces, high ceilings, a dying market driving down rental costs. A vacuum waiting for something to emerge to productively use this formerly valuable space. Some genius came up with the idea of inflatables, kid's parties and Ice Cream cake.

Well, this little history of the rise of the bounce house economy is all a little precursor to say damn, ain't it crazy how many damn birthday parties you end up navigating on so many Saturday and Sunday mornings, afternoons and evenings now. It's worth a double damn. I was at our local house of bouncy fun for dinner on Saturday and lunch on Sunday this past weekend.

It's a strange ecosystem, the class birthday party. Clearly these are many of the kids your kids will be growing up with. More pressing however is the parents. The kids occupy themselves at these events quite naturally. It's us parents who have the true dilemma of figuring out how to be around others.

Maybe it's not everyone. Maybe it's just me who finds this so exceedingly forced and awkward. I'm pretty sure my own discomfort is projecting outward and making others uncomfortable. I mean, I have to look pretty sketchy, avoiding all eye contact, standing away from everyone, thinking I should be social for my kids' sake then hovering around conversations I'm not meant to be a part of. It's so awkward.

Here are some of the parents you will see at your kid's friend's birthday parties.

THE GHOSTER - You may never see this dad or mom. They would prefer to simply slow the car down and have their child tuck and roll onto the sidewalk and into the fun of the bounce house. Most at a minimum stay long enough to sign papers ensuring they won't sue if there is an accidental dismemberment. Next time you see them is when the lights come on after the birthday boy or girl has blown out the candles. Or shortly thereafter. Or shortly after that. *NOTE: Given any inkling that it is acceptable to disappear for the duration I am this dad.*

THE HIGH STYLE PARENT - It is Saturday, late morning. Either you haven't slept and look remarkably put together considering you're wearing the same clothes you wore for date night last night, and it was like anniversary date night, a round number no less, or you have put a lot of effort in to looking good at the strip mall bounce house hut. Also I'm suddenly made hyper self-conscious by my laughably dated, though equally imperfectly fitting cargo's and maybe I should have skipped the Crocs. Yep. I'm that dad. I apologize for many things, but not comfort. It's my prerogative as a middle aged dad.

THE LURKER- Standing at the outskirts, watching his kid nonstop, avoiding any and all contact with the other parents. This is always a dad in my experience, but I'm sure there are some moms as well. Just drifting to zero population centers in the grown up sections. I am this man though I'm getting better.

PTA PARENT - You know the type. The one who has followed through on all those things we say we'll do when our kids get into school. This parent is pretty typically very nice and I'm thankful when they approach with a topic to discuss. I am not this parent. I may judge this parent silently as a defense mechanism as they are doing it right, which highlights my shortcomings.

OVERLY ENTHUSIASTIC DAD - This guy. You know this guy. 'He's just a big kid!' is something someone who was likely annoyed with him said once and he has since taken it on as his identity. He is way too much. Sucks that my kid can't stop talking about him and how awesome he is. I'm not jealous.. You're jealous!

THE HOVERER - This parent is on the opposite end of the spectrum from The Ghoster. They are in a constant state of risk assessment and periodically intervening to avoid certain calamities that never happen. I know some of these folks and there hearts are definitely in the right place. Their anxiety, however, can run interference.

SCREEN DEMON - Finally. My tribe. We are determined to avoid interaction with any adults. We are Facebooking, Tweeting, Snapchatting and Gramming all while determinedly maintaining a scowl that tries hard to say, 'this is very important work I'm doing. Important and private. I'm sorry I can't talk, but me and my phone are saving the world.

Pick your strategy wisely folks! You may just have to maintain this personality for the duration of your child's schooling!

I Don't Have The Words

I don't know that I will ever be able to fully articulate how I love my kids. Were it a quantifiable thing I'd give you a number. As it is I don't think any sophisticated adult has ever improved on the simple claim made by all of us lucky enough to have been loved as a child who have spread our arms wide and said, 'I love you this much!'

Charlie is the sweetest boy and he will stop us to make sure we are listening, in the middle of getting ready for bed or when we are cooking or whenever, to tell us, 'I love you. You're the best daddy.' or, 'Mommy, I love you more than anything ever!'

'Oh, Charlie.' I gasp, 'I love you so much, you are the most wonderful boy.'

I wish words were more evolved. I wish our minds, our full creativity could describe what flows through you as a parent. All of it is extreme. The frustrations, the joys the exhaustion's and elation's. The simple act of falling for your child, for me an act that happened in an instant opens a vein you didn't know you had. It pours from you in every way you can imagine.

I didn't appreciate the love I was given as a child, not fully at least, until I discovered it from the other side. Until I looked intently at my own kid and marveled and recoiled and felt the bond between us so deeply that it seemed I could reach out and hold it.

Teddy is my little man and I can't get over his curiosity. He's trying all the time that his brother is around to compete, a thing that looks different in a younger brother than an older one. His focus primarily is on his big brother but his quiet moments are the ones that steal my heart. He can smile when your head shares a pillow with his and he wants to tell you about all the things he is thinking. About his ideas and plans, about how much he loves mommy and Charlie and me. He builds big and little bridges to you and everyone one at a time. It's magic.

On the other side of this newfound entity of love for my kids is an equally newfound fear. One that could only exist in relation to my fondness for these boys. I'm terribly afraid of random tragedy now. While they have opened me up, have cracked the shell around my heart, they have also made me a vigilant hawk. See, I'm now and forevermore aware that there is something infinitely more tragic that can happen than there ever was prior to now.

The first week it paralyzed us to a degree. We had no idea that there was something so awful as the fears of a parent before they hit us. People can't wait to tell you about the lack of sleep and the magic of babies. They don't tell you that the most tragic of ends now comes to reside in your resting imagination.

I never so feared my own death before knowing that it would affect my own kids. It never occurred to me to think of it. Now if Karen so much as has a cold I'm worried, only for a moment at a time, but I worry there's something bigger hidden in her cough. If I'm making dinner and she's picking up the kids and they are a few minutes late my brain arrives, in an instant, at a place where I can imagine all three of them, struggling in an overturned car, or thrown from the car, scared and alone in their final moments. I know. IT'S AWFUL!!

But as quick as it comes it disappears and I'm back to worrying about whether or not I should use the last of the celery as it's Charlie's go to and whether or not T will eat the string beans or should I not bother to make them.

I don't know what the word would be to describe these things, these rushes between otherworldly levels of joy and dread and monotony, but there should be a word. It seems to be a universal feeling and across the board it seems unknowable until the instant you fall for that kid and unshakable from that point forward.